JANE EYRE

By Charlotte Brontë
Adapted by Nick Lane

Published by Playdead Press 2019

© Nick Lane 2019

Nick Lane has asserted his rights under the Copyright, Design and Patents Act, 1988, to be identified as the authors of this work.

A CIP catalogue record for this book is available from the British Library.

ISBN 978-1-910067-83-3

Playdead Press
www.playdeadpress.com

Jane Eyre

By Charlotte Brontë

Adapted by Nick Lane

**Produced by Blackeyed Theatre
in association with South Hill Park Arts Centre**

Cast

Jane Eyre	**Kelsey Short**
Edward Rochester/ Mr Brocklehurst	**Ben Warwick**
Mrs Fairfax / Bertha Mason / Aunt Reed / Mary Rivers	**Camilla Simson**
Blanche Ingram / Georgianna Reed / Helen Burns / Adèle Varens / Diana Rivers	**Eleanor Toms**
St John Rivers / John Reed / Mr Mason	**Oliver Hamilton**

Artistic Team

Writer	**Nick Lane**
Composer	**George Jennings**
Director/Producer	**Adrian McDougall**
Musical Director	**Ellie Verkerk**
Movement Director	**Sammy Fonfe**
Fight and Intimacy Director	**Enric Ortuño**
Assistant Director	**Lucy Fennell**
Set Designer	**Victoria Spearing**
Costume Designer	**Naomi Gibbs**
Lighting Designer	**Alan Valentine**
Company Stage Manager	**Benjamin Smith**
Set Construction	**Russell Pearn / Steve Spearing / Jane O'Sullivan**
Properties	**Sophie Spearing**

Cast

Kelsey Short | *Jane Eyre*

Kelsey trained at Rose Bruford.

Theatre credits include *Class* (Spur of the Moment), *F*cking Life Mate* (JamesArts Productions), *Interrupted* (JW3), *Teeth, Shoes* (Theatre 503), *Between a Man and a Woman* (JamesArts Productions), *Broken* (The White Bear), *Another Day* (A Friend of a Friend Productions).

Screen credits include *Between a Man and a Woman* and *Chip* (JamesArts Productions).

Kelsey writes spoken word poetry and is a skilled puppeteer.

Ben Warwick | *Mr Rochester / Mr Brocklehurst*

Ben trained at The Guildhall School of Music and Drama. He last appeared with Blackeyed Theatre as Victor Frankenstein.

Theatre credits include *Hamlet* (English Touring Theatre), *The Deep Blue Sea* (Watford Palace), *Pentecost, The Oedipus Plays* (Royal National Theatre), *Les Liaisons Dangereuses, A Midsummer Night's Dream* (Theatre Royal York), *House And Garden* (Royal Theatre Northampton), *Look Back In Anger* (Lichfield Garrick), *Arms & The Man, The Captain's Tiger, Saint's Day, The Road To Ruin, Skeletons* (Orange Tree), *The Trench* (Les Enfants Terribles – National and International tours and Southwark Playhouse), *The Marquise* (Bill Kenwright), *Macbeth* (US Tour), *Miss Julie*

(Soho Theatre), *Moliere Or The League Of Hypocrites* (Finborough), *Cock* (Folktearten Gothenberg), *The Seagull, The Picture of Dorian Gray* (tour of Russia for Arterie), *Great Expectations, She Stoops to Conquer, The Bandwagon, Charley's Aunt, Henry IV pt.1, Hard Times, Our Town, Room Service, Tons Of Money, David Copperfield* (Farnham Rep).

Feature films include *Blood Moon, War Game, Canakkale Yolun Sonu*. TV includes *Mary Queen of Scots* (BBC) *Emmerdale* (ITV), *The Big Picture, Five Years*.

benwarwickactor.com

Camilla Simson | *Mrs Fairfax / Bertha Mason / Aunt Reed / Mary Rivers*

Camilla trained at Elmhurst Ballet School and Webber Douglas Academy of Dramatic Art.

Theatre credits include *The Merchant of Venice* (Bedouin Shakespeare Co. at the Globe, Rome), *A Bunch of Amateurs*

(Theatre On The Coast, Southwold), *The Little Things* (The Latchmere Theatre), *Hounds of the Baskervilles* (Greenwich Theatre with SellaDoor), *Blithe Spirit* (Hever Castle Festival), *Fred and Gladys* (The Landor), *Thin Toes* (The Pleasance), *The Treason Show* (The Komedia, Brighton), *Valparaiso* (The Old Red Lion), *Crystal Clear* (The Landor & Edinburgh Festival), *Talking Heads – Her Big Chance* (Wimbledon Theatre), *Dick Whittington* (Cambridge Arts Theatre), *Lady Windermere's Fan* (Bill Kenwright, National Tour), *Love Off The Shelf* (Harrogate and Nuffield Theatres), *Alice in Wonderland* (Nuffield Theatre), *Shakers* (Liverpool Playhouse), *Bertie, The Life of Vesta Tilley* (Alexandra Theatre Birmingham).

Television and Film credits include *King Of Chaos* (Stone City Films, C4), *London's Burning* (ITV), *Are You Ready For Love* (Carnaby Films) and *Funny Bones* (Suntrust Films).

Eleanor Toms | *Blanche Ingram / Georgianna Reed / Helen Burns / Adèle Varens / Diana Rivers*

Eleanor trained at the Guildford School of Acting and graduated in 2016.

Theatre credits include *The Secret Garden* (The Minack Theatre), *Macbeth* (This is my Theatre), *A Dickensian Christmas* (Ha-Hum-Ah Theatre), *Astley's Astounding Adventures* (New Vic), *Fiddler on the Roof* (Frinton Summer Theatre), *Treasure Island* (New Vic), *Blue Stockings* (Cockpit Theatre), *The Lost Boy Peter Pan* (Catford Broadway, for Action to the Word), *A Little Night Music* (Frinton Summer Theatre), *Paper Hearts* (Upstairs at the Gatehouse and Hamburg).

Oliver Hamilton | *St John Rivers / John Reed / Mr Mason*

Oliver trained at the Royal Central School of Speech and Drama having previously graduated from Manchester University.

Theatre credits include *Maggie May* (Liverpool Everyman), *Crossroads* (Actors Church, Covent Garden), *A Christmas Carol* (Windsor Castle) and *Blue Into Gold* (Collfest, London).

Theatre whilst training included *The Wonderful World of Dissocia, Parade, A Bomb on Broadway, Sweeney Todd, Beweep Outcast, A Clockwork Orange* and *Kiss of the Spider Woman.*

CREATIVE

Nick Lane | Adapter

Nick's previous adaptations for Blackeyed Theatre include *Sherlock Holmes: the Sign of Four* and *The Strange Case of Dr. Jekyll & Mr. Hyde.* Other adaptations include *Dark Winter* (E52), *Frankenstein* (Theatre Mill), *The Wakefield Mysteries* (Theatre Royal Wakefield), *1984* (Northern Broadsides), *Lady Chatterley's Lover* and a co-adaptation (with John Godber) of *Moby Dick* (Hull Truck). Original adult plays include: *The Derby McQueen Affair* (York Theatre Royal), *My Favourite Summer, Blue Cross Xmas* and *Me & Me Dad* (Hull Truck), *Housebound, Hopeless Romantics* – co-written with Fiona Wass and *Seconds Out* (Reform), *Royal Flush* and *Odd Job Men* (Rich Seam Theatre), *Murder at Berrington* – co-written with Fiona Wass and *The Goal* (Hereford Courtyard).

Nick is also an accomplished children's playwright – his credits include: *A Christmas Carol, Beauty & The Beast, The Hunchback of Notre Dame* and *The Snow Queen* (Hull Truck); *Pinocchio, A Scarborough Christmas Carol* and *Alice in Wonderland* (SJT); *Snow White* and *Little Red Riding Hood* (York Theatre Royal); *The Elves & The Shoemaker* (Hereford Courtyard); and *Hansel & Gretel* (Pilot). His original work for children includes *Ginger Jones and the Sultan's Eye* (Polka / Drum Theatre Plymouth / York Theatre Royal), *'Twas the Night before Christmas, When Santa Got Stuck in the Fridge* and *A Christmas Fairytale* (Hull Truck).

Nick's directing credits outside of his own work include *The Glass Menagerie, Departures, Life's A Beach, Studs, Beef,*

Amateur Girl, Lucky Sods and *Ring Around the Humber* (Hull Truck), *April in Paris, Two, September in the Rain* and *Little Italy* (York Theatre Royal), *Don't Dribble on the Dragon* and *There Was an Old Lady who Swallowed a Fly* (PTC).

George Jennings | Composer

Graduating from the Guildford School of Acting in 2013, George is an actor, musician and composer.

His composition credits include *The Archive of Educated Hearts* (Lion House Theatre), which was awarded a Scotsman Fringe First at the Edinburgh Fringe 2018, *Michael Morpurgo's King Arthur* (UK Tour), *Macbeth* (South Hill Park), *From Dust* (Gilded Balloon), *A Pocketful of Grimm's* (UK Tour), *Acedian Pirates* (Theatre503), *Night Creature* (Adelaide Fringe), *Romeo & Juliet* (South Hill Park), and *This was the World and I was King (*HookHitch Theatre), which was nominated by Musical Theatre Network for best score at the Edinburgh Fringe 2013, before touring the UK and enjoying runs at The Brockley Jack and The Arts Theatre.

George has also written scores for various short films and podcasts.

As an actor, he has appeared in productions at Shakespeare's Globe, in the West End and in numerous regional theatres around the country, as well as screen appearances on the BBC and History Channel.

georgejenningsmusic.com

Adrian McDougall | Director and Producer

Adrian is the founder and Artistic Director of Blackeyed Theatre. He grew up in Berkshire, studying modern languages at Southampton University, going on to work in marketing and PR, before becoming an actor, theatre producer and director.

As a director, his credits include – for Blackeyed Theatre – the award-nominated world premiere of *The Beekeeper* and national tours of *Oh What A Lovely War*, *Teechers* and *Alfie*, as well as productions of *Brassed Off* and *House And Garden* (for South Hill Park).

Since Blackeyed Theatre's very first production, *Effie's Burning*, he has produced 20 national tours, including the world premiere of Steven Berkoff's *Oedipus*, brand new stage adaptations of *The Sign Of Four*, *The Strange case of Dr Jekyll & Mr Hyde*, *Frankenstein*, *The Great Gatsby* and *Dracula*, as well as UK tours of *The Caretaker*, *The Resistible Rise of Arturo Ui*, *Mother Courage And Her Children*, *The Caucasian Chalk Circle*, *The Trial* and *Not About Heroes*.

Also for Blackeyed Theatre, he has commissioned original productions of *A Christmas Carol*, *Peter Pan* and *Beauty & The Beast*.

He has also worked as an actor, touring the UK with Blackeyed Theatre, Oddsocks Productions, Premiere Stage Productions and the Phoenix Theatre Company.

He lives in Wokingham with his wife and two young children.

Ellie Verkerk | Musical Director

Ellie graduated from the Royal College of Music as a pianist, accompanist and orchestral musician, and has worked with a broad variety of musicians, singers and singer-songwriters, from London's West End to recording sessions, cabarets, weddings and beyond.

She was the assistant to the conductor and production assistant to the film director for *Celebrating John Lord* (Royal

Albert Hall), she has worked as a keys player for *Jersey Boys* (Prince Edward Theatre) and is currently Cover Musical Director for Six: the Musical (Arts Theatre, West End). Her work as Musical Director includes *Beauty and the Beast, Oh What A Lovely War, Mother Courage* and *Dracula* (Blackeyed Theatre), and *Cabaret in the Cellar Bar* (South Hill Park). Her work as Assistant Musical Director includes *Kerrigan-Lowdermilk LIVE* (St. James Theatre), and *All I Want for Christmas...* (Julie Atherton, St James Theatre). Recording and session work includes *My Parade (*Stephanie Fearon), and singer-songwriters *Dear Pariah* and *Buswell*. She has appeared as a trumpet player in music videos, and conducted a symphony orchestra at the Shepherd's Bush Empire as part of the *Underground Orchestra Challenge* with Sean Buswell.

Ellie is a passionate supporter of young people, teaching and supporting those who aspire to work professionally in the creative arts industry, and works at the *Read Dance and Theatre College* (Reading, Berkshire). In addition to her musical work, Ellie is also a massage therapist, specialising in the treatment of musicians and performers, and works regularly with people with special needs.

www.EllieVerkerk.com.

Sammy Fonfe | Movement Director

Sammy gained a MA in Creative Musical Theatre Practice at Arts Educational School, where she is now the dance tutor on the BA Acting course.

Credits whilst training include Assistant Choreographer / Director on *Evita* for the opening of Andrew Lloyd Webber's new theatre and Associate Choreographer on *Kiss of the Spider Woman* and The *Spelling Bee.*

Credits as Choreography and Movement Director include *Beauty and the Beast* (Redhill), *Judas Excalibur and Love and Information* (Arts Education Theatre), *Snow White* (PHA, The Harlequin Theatre), *Romeo and Juliet* (RBL, Greenwich Theatre), *Twelfth Night* (RBL), *Henry* (RBL), *From Up Here* (Tristan Bates Theatre), *A Night of the Musicals* (UK Tour, resident Choreographer), *Somewhere Over The West Way* (Edinburgh Festival and Portobello), *Sweet FA* (New Theatre Royal, Portsmouth), *The Tenth Kingdom* (Carnival Films), *Dangerous Corner* (UK Tour), *Lisa Scott Lee on Tour* (Asia & UK Tour), *Hot Mikado* (The Wilde Theatre), *A View from the Bridge* (Lyric Hammersmith), Dear Edwina (The Lost Theatre, Assistant Choreographer).

Sammy is Managing Director of the Berkshire Theatre Company. Where they give new generations opportunities to learn with professionals and perform in theatres throughout Berkshire.

www.berkshiretheatrecompany.co.uk

Enric Ortuño | Fight and Intimacy Director

Enric is a certified Stage Combat Teacher by the British Academy of Stage and Screen Combat. He holds a 4yr BA in Musical Theatre from the Spanish Conservatoire of Dramatic Art and an MA in Movement Studies from the Royal Central School of Speech and Drama.

Enric is the resident combat teacher at Drama Studio London, Italia Conti, Kogan Academy of Dramatic Art and the Academy of Performance Training (Guildford) and teaches regularly at RADA, Central School of Speech and Drama and has taught workshops in Spain, Canada, USA and Germany.

His credits include *The Weatherman* (Park Theatre), *The Drag* (Arcola Theatre), *Boris: World King* (Trafalgar Studios),

Croydon Avengers (Ovalhouse Theatre), *The Amber Trap* (Theatre 503), *Love me Now* (Tristan Bates Theatre), *Escape the Scaffold* (Theatre 503), *Firecracker* (Ovalhouse Theatre), *Verdi's Macbeth* (Iford Arts), *The Autumn Garden* (Jermyn Street Theatre), *Jekyll & Hyde* (Arrows & Traps Theatre Company), *The 3 Musketeers* (ElevenOne Theatre), *Treasure Island* (Oxford Theatre Guild), *The Ladykillers* (Wokingham Theatre), *Men Should Weep* (Landor Theatre), *Candy Cansino Checks In* (Landor Theatre), *Othello* (Barons Court Theatre), *Dangerous Giant Animals* (Underbelly Edinburgh), *Days of Significance* (Landor Theatre), *Monster* (Worklight Theatre), *Titus Andronicus* and *Othello* (Smooth Faced Gentlemen).

Lucy Fennell | Assistant Director

Lucy completed her English degree and PGCE in Canterbury and went on to teach English and Drama in secondary schools before becoming a theatre maker, director and performer. She has trained extensively in improvisation and is a founding member of Impromptu Shakespeare, with whom she has performed in a number of festivals and national tours. She recently completed a residency with The Bristol Improv Theatre where she devised and directed *Is it improvised, does it matter?* an exploration of the divide between scripted theatre and improvisation.

Lucy is an experienced facilitator and has worked extensively as a director of young people in her role as Education officer at The Point and The Berry Theatre. She directed *The Tempest* and *Henry V* (as part of HLF funded Agincourt 600) and was the Youth Theatre Director at the Berry Theatre. Her directing credits include: *The Little Mermaid*, *The Secret Garden* and *James and the Giant Peach*. She also produced *Adventures of the Improvised Sherlock Holmes*'s 2018 sell out Edinburgh Fringe run.

Lucy has taught theatre and performance at a range of universities including: University of Creative Arts, University of Kent and York University and currently teaches at Artemis College whilst also tutoring English for GCSE and A-Level.

She has performed in *Bumper Blyton: The improvised Adventure*, and you can spot her in the BAFTA award-winning educational series *History Bombs*.

Victoria Spearing | Set Designer

Victoria trained at Bretton Hall in Theatre Design and Technology. She is resident designer at South Hill Park Arts Centre with whom she won the award for Best Staging / Set at the 2019 Great British Pantomime Awards for their production of *Dick Whittington And His Cat*.

This will be the 21st design for Blackeyed Theatre, from *The Caretaker* to the highly acclaimed tours of *Not About Heroes*, *Dracula* and *Teechers*. Her design for *The Beekeeper* was nominated for the Best Set Design in the 2012 Off West End Theatre Awards.

For South Hill Park she has designed the last twelve pantomimes, as well as a range of in-house productions, including *Brassed Off*, *Stepping Out*, *Blood Brothers*, *Calendar Girls* and *Oh What A Lovely War*. She also redesigned South Hill Park's Wilde Theatre Bar and Foyer to create a new performance space.

Her design work for other companies includes the world premiere of *A Little History of the World* (Watermill Theatre), *The Dumb Waiter, Miss Julie, Waiting for Godot, Race* and *The Nativity that Goes Wrong* (Reading Rep), *Journey's End,*

Dancing at Lughnasa, The Madness of George III, Three Men in a Boat and *Birdsong* (Original Theatre Company), *Lotty's War* (Giddy Ox), *Loserville* (Youth Music Theatre), *The History Boys* and *Danny the Champion of the World* (London Contemporary Theatre), as well as various Christmas shows for The Castle Wellingborough.

Naomi Gibbs | Costume Designer

Naomi is a costume designer from Southsea, in residency at the New Theatre Royal Portsmouth where she leads a team of freelance makers', building costumes for clients in the entertainment and music industries. She's been designing for stage for over a decade and working with Blackeyed a theatre since 2016. In 2009 Naomi set up her costume design business 'Society Belle' which has recently expanded to form a collective of skilled professionals under the name 'Portsmouth Costumiers'.

Costume design credits include; *Moon Language* (Stopgap Dance Company), Hypozeuxsis (FunkFormat), *The Strange Case of Doctor Jekyll and Mr Hyde, Teechers, Sherlock Holmes and the Sign of Four,* (Blackeyed Theatre), *Beauty and the Beast, Peter Pan, The Nutcracker* (New Theatre Royal, Portsmouth), Grimm Tales, Aladdin (South Hill Park).

www.societybelle.co.uk

Alan Valentine | Lighting Designer

Alan's previous work for Blackeyed Theatre includes *Teechers, The Madness of George III, Mother Courage* and *Misery*.

His other lighting design credits include; for Original Theatre – *The Importance of Being Earnest, The Madness of George III,*

Dancing at Lughnasa, Journey's End, Shakespeare's R&J, See How They Run and *Twelfth Night.*

For Youth Music Theatre UK (now BYMT) – *Paperboy, A Winter's Tale, Help! Get me out of this Musical, A Teenage Opera, The Great Gatsby, Fagin, A Beggar's Opera, Mort, Macbeth, Tess of the D'Urbevilles, Out there* and *Loserville the Musical.*

For South Hill Park Arts Centre, Alan's credits include *Private Peaceful, Romeo and Juliet, Henry V, Macbeth, The Magic Finger, James and the Giant Peach, Just So, Seussical the Musical, High School Musical, The Importance of Being Earnest, Noughts and Crosses, From up Here (with* Perfect Pitch) and the large-scale outdoor event *Wild Fire.*

He recently worked on *Crazy for You* for Mountview Academy of Theatre Arts, and occasionally works as a relighter for James Finnemore (*Terra)* and Hofesh Shechter Company, touring productions of *Sun, Political Mother, Barbarians* and *Show.*

Benjamin Smith | Company Stage Manager

Benjamin graduated from the Royal Welsh College of Music and Drama in Stage Management and Technical Theatre.

Since graduating, Benjamin has worked in a range of roles. His stage / production management credits include *Vulvarine* and *Unfortunate* (Fat Rascal Theatre), *Austen* (Harker Studios), the MA Actor / Muso Showcase (Guildford School of Acting) and *The Worst Little Warehouse In London.*

Benjamin's sound design credits include *Word Gets Around* (RCT Theatre), *Memory of Water* and *Oh Go My Man* (ALRA North) and *Alternative Routes* (National Dance Company of Wales).

His lighting credits include Lighting Assistant for *2023* (Illumine Theatre), *Austen* (Harker Studios) and *The 39 Steps* (Fourth Wall Theatre).

This is Benjamin's first show with Blackeyed Theatre and he's very excited to be involved.

BLA⊙KEYED
THEATRE

Blackeyed Theatre has been creating exciting, sustainable theatre throughout the UK since 2004. We have taken our work to over a hundred different theatres across England, Scotland and Wales, from 50 seat studios to 1000 seat opera houses.

Central to everything we do is our desire both to challenge and engage artists and audiences. As a company that receives minimal funding, we are proof that commercially successful theatre can still be innovative and can still surprise. We believe that only by balancing a desire to push artistic boundaries with an appreciation of what audiences have a desire to see do you create theatre that is truly sustainable, both commercially and artistically.

We bring together artists with a genuine passion for the work they produce, offering a theatrical experience that's both artistically excellent, affordable and accessible.

Our previous national tours include *Sherlock Holmes: The Sign Of Four*, *The Strange Case of Dr Jekyll And Mr Hyde* (Robert Louis Stevenson, adapted by Nick Lane), *Frankenstein* (Mary Shelley, adapted by John Ginman), *The Great Gatsby* (F. Scott Fitzgerald, adapted by Stephen Sharkey), *Not About Heroes* (Stephen MacDonald), *Dracula* (Bram Stoker, adapted by John Ginman), *Teechers* (John Godber), *Mother Courage And Her Children* (Bertolt Brecht), *The Trial* (Steven Berkoff), *The Caucasian Chalk Circle* (Bertolt Brecht), *Alfie* (Bill Naughton), *The Cherry Orchard* (Anton Chekhov), *Oh What a Lovely War* (Joan Littlewood), the world premiere of *Oedipus* (Steven Berkoff) and *The Resistible Rise of Arturo Ui* (Bertolt Brecht).

In 2011, Blackeyed Theatre launched Pulse, a new-writing competition. The winning script, *The Beekeeper*, enjoyed a three-week London Fringe run, receiving three OFFIE nominations, including Best New Play.

The company is resident at South Hill Park Arts Centre in Bracknell, where we continue to create accessible theatre that challenges expectations, furthering our reputation as one of the UK's leading touring theatre companies.

"One of the most innovative, audacious companies working in contemporary English theatre"
The Stage

www.blackeyedtheatre.co.uk
@blackeyedtheatr

South Hill Park Arts Centre

South Hill Park Arts Centre has been at the creative heart of Berkshire for over 40 years. This picturesque 18th century mansion house in Bracknell houses two theatres, a dance studio, visual arts spaces, artists in residence, a comedy club, resident associate companies, a digital media suite, and a cinema.

Across our varied creative spaces we bring 300 shows, events and films to our audiences each year, alongside a busy programme of over 250 courses and workshops. To improve access and representation of young people within the arts, South Hill Park also supports a group of young producers, aged between 14 and 25 years, who plan and devise arts activities and provision for other young people in the local area.

South Hill Park collaborates with theatre makers and companies in a variety of ways. The artistic vision of the centre includes the support and development of, and collaboration with many of its associate companies including its resident company Blackeyed Theatre Company. Many of these touring productions begin their artistic inception and development at South Hill Park.

South Hill Park also works closely with its other associate companies including Chrysalis, Hit the Mark, Luke Brown, Peer Productions, Single Shoe Productions and Theatre Re.

To find out more sign up to our newsletter:

Southhillpark.org.uk
facebook.com/SouthHillParkArtsCentre
twitter.com/southhillpark
Instagram.com/southhillpark

South Hill Park Arts Centre
Ringmead
Bracknell
Berkshire, RG12 7PA

South Hill Park Trust Limited
Registered Charity No: 265656

A note from the Adapter

Do you remember that feeling when you were a kid, of standing at the edge of a swimming pool for the first time, arm-bands on, watching the water ripple and dance and daring yourself to jump in? That curious mixture of excitement and nerves? Remember that? Well... when Adrian asked me about adapting *Jane Eyre* I experienced something not dissimilar!

The excitement's pretty easy to explain. Charlotte Bronte's masterpiece has stood the test of time and continues to speak to readers about the importance of being true to yourself, about determination in the face of unspeakable odds, and the redemptive power of true love no matter the cost. What writer wouldn't want to explore those characters and find their own way to bring the book to the stage?

Personally when adapting a book I've never wanted to massively subvert audience expectations – *Jane Eyre* is intricate, terrifying, delicate, heart-breaking and beautiful (sometimes in the same sentence) and I hope I've captured some of that. It's also a remarkably dense and detailed story; what you're trying to do is retain the essence of the writing while streamlining a little. Those who know the novel well will recognise certain minor changes and I cross my fingers that they aren't too upset!

And the nerves? Well they were about Jane herself. She's such an iconic character; so beloved by readers all over the world. If I get her wrong, I thought... it was my mum's favourite book (well, that and *Pride & Prejudice*) and she would have never forgiven me if I didn't do her justice.

A very good friend told me not too long ago that Jane is such a wonderful character because she is different for every reader. I hope I've found your Jane.

Nick Lane

Dramatis Personae

ACTOR ONE   Miss Jane Eyre, *a free spirit*

ACTOR TWO   Mr. Edward Rochester, *a complicated soul*
Also: Mr. Brocklehurst (a schoolmaster)

ACTOR THREE   Mrs. Fairfax, *a housekeeper*
Also: Aunt Reed (an aunt to Jane), Miss Temple (a teacher), Mrs. Ingram (mother to Blanche), Bertha Mason (the first wife of Mr. Rochester), Mary Rivers (a good Christian soul)

ACTOR FOUR   Miss Blanche Ingram, *an unmarried beauty*
Also: Georgiana Reed (a cousin to Jane), Helen Burns (Jane's school friend), Adèle Varens (Mr. Rochester's French ward), Diana Rivers (a good Christian soul)

ACTOR FIVE   Mr. St. John Rivers, *a man of God*
Also: John Reed (a cousin to Jane), William (a servant), Mr. Mason (a mysterious visitor), Coachman (a coachman)

Author's note

As with all adaptations I am grateful for any assistance that might keep me focussed on the original creator's vision. In this instance I'd like to mention Laura Turner, a writer whose own terrific version of Jane Eyre provided great inspiration... and Tabitha Grove, whose knowledge of the text and insight into both the eponymous heroine and Charlotte Bronte herself was nothing short of breathtaking. Thanks, Tab. NL

Act One. *The stage is an abstract space, a skeletal structure suggesting the burnt remains of a grand mansion – Thornfield Hall – dominates. On the back wall hangs a cyc. The floor is fire-damaged floorboards. Around the edge of the space, marking the playing area are burned objects – items of furniture, clothing &c. Sections of furniture next to blistered door-frames provide naturalistic entrances. The chairs within the space are both mismatched and equally charred. One chair has a charred book on it as the play begins. At FOH clearance lights fade to black and the company enters. As lights come up a single voice begins to sing, other voices and instruments joining in as the play progresses.*

COMPANY

Speak of the North! A lonely Moor
Silent and dark and tractless swells,
The waves of some wild streamlet pour
Hurriedly through its ferny dells

Profoundly still the twilight air
Lifeless the landscape, so we deem
Til like a phantom gliding near
A stag bends down to drink the stream.

And far away a mountain zone,
A cold-white waste of snow drifts lies
And one star, large and soft and lone,
Silently lights the unclouded skies.

JANE is revealed, looking around the charred remains. She moves downstage, music underscoring as the rest of the company repeat her name and begin to over-layer lines and words from her story.

THREE   *(Whispered)* Jane.

FIVE	*(Whispered)* Jane.
FOUR	*(Whispered)* Jane Eyre.
TWO	*(Whispered)* Jane.
FOUR	*(Whispered)* Jane. Eyre.
FIVE	*(Whispered)* Jane.
TWO	*(As ROCHESTER)* Do you never laugh, Miss Eyre?
FOUR	*(Whispered)* Jane Eyre.
THREE	*(As AUNT REED)* Disobedient child!
TWO	*(Whispered)* Jane.
FOUR	*(As BLANCHE)* Dreary looking thing.
FIVE	*(As BROCKLEHURST)* Wicked. And a liar!
TWO	*(Whispered)* Jane.
THREE	*(As FAIRFAX)* We should have told you the truth; I know that.
FIVE	*(As ST. JOHN)* You scorn only God.
THREE	*(Whispered)* Jane.
TWO	*(As ROCHESTER)* Solemn creature.
FIVE	*(Whispered)* Jane Eyre.

The underscore continues. JANE looks out and addresses the audience.

JANE	*(To audience)* Everything has changed and nothing has. The view from this window is wilder... and more beautiful. I am alone but not lonely. I'm not cold. I'm not warm. I'm home.

FIVE becomes JOHN REED, JANE's hateful cousin.

	Every fractured wall and shattered windowpane... every burned and blackened stick of furniture still offers more kindness, more beauty... more *hope* than anywhere I have lived. And I did live here, reader. Truly, I *lived*.

JOHN REED's voice is cruel and searching; he is looking for her.

REED	Rat...?
JANE	*(To audience)* When I consider my youth; my dread of solitude...
REED	Where are you, rat?
JANE	*(To audience)* How others preyed upon that dread...
REED	Come out! You know I'll find you...
JANE	*(To audience)* I wonder how the girl I was might marvel...
REED	Are you in... here?
JANE	*(To audience)* ...to learn of the woman she'd become. How she might have dealt with her Aunt Reed...

REED   Are you in… here?

JANE   *(To audience)* …or her cousins; Georgiana… and John.

Lights change. Music fades. We have left Thornfield and are now in Gateshead Hall.

REED   Draw every set of curtains in the library, would you?

JANE   *(To audience)* I am a child again.

REED   Think you're so clever. don't you, rat?

JANE   *(To audience)* It is my birthday.

REED   Answer me!

JANE   They were already drawn.

REED   Liar!

JOHN REED raises his hand as if to strike JANE. JANE naturally flinches, which makes him smile. JOHN REED snatches the book and holds it to JANE's face.

     What's this?

JANE   Bewick's History of British Birds.

REED   This is our book, not yours. Are you reading it?

JANE   Of course.

REED   I wondered why you hadn't joined us on the walk.

JANE	I wasn't invited.
REED	How *dare* you speak that way? Mama looked for you.
JANE	I was in my room all morning.
REED	Liar!

He raises his hand again. JANE flinches again.

	You tell one more lie, rat, and there'll be punishment.
JANE	May I have the book?
REED	No. I want it. Think I might throw it on the fire.
JANE	Please; don't!
REED	Oh; oh... you like it, do you?
JANE	Yes!
REED	How much do you like it?
JANE	Enough for you not to burn it!
REED	Hold out your hands then; I'll give it to you. *(Calling off)* Georgiana? I'm giving cousin Jane a birthday present. *(To JANE)* How old are you today?
JANE	Ten.
REED	Then you deserve ten favours. Close your eyes.

JANE	No.
REED	Close them.
JANE	You'll hit me like yesterday.
REED	I didn't.
JANE	Like every day.
REED	Liar!

This time JOHN REED strikes JANE with the book. It's the final straw for JANE who launches herself at JOHN REED with a roar and starts hitting him. He stumbles to the floor and she's astride him, pummelling him and shouting:

JANE	Wicked, cruel boy! You're like a murderer! A slave driver! You're like the Roman Emperors!
REED	Get – get off me!

At this point FOUR enters as GEORGIANA and gasps. JANE continues to attack JOHN REED. He calls to his sister…

	She started it!
GEORGIANA	Nasty little thing.
JANE	He's lying!
REED	Agh! I never lie! Aagh!
GEORGIANA	*(Calling off)* Mama! Come quickly! Jane's gone mad!

THREE enters as AUNT REED.

AUNT REED   I'm here.

Music. Upon hearing her Aunt's voice JANE knows the game is up. She stands and moves away from JOHN REED, who crawls across the floor making a great show of his injuries, then smiling cruelly at JANE as he cowers at his mother's skirts, until:

                    Oh get up, John; you're fourteen.

JOHN REED stands and positions himself behind his mother.

GEORGIANA   You mustn't be angry with John, mama –
                    I saw the whole affair. Jane turned on him
                    like a wild animal.

AUNT REED now rounds on JANE.

AUNT REED   *(To JANE)* There was a time I might
                    have expected more, Jane Eyre. A little
                    gratitude, perhaps. Instead I see nothing
                    but spite and malice.

JANE opens her mouth to defend herself but AUNT REED holds up a finger.

                    I shouldn't need to go through this with
                    you again, but you've left me no choice.
                    Stand up straight.

At this, GEORGIANA and JOHN REED begin to both smile and offer looks of shame. It is not the first time JANE has been subjected to this humiliation.

                    Now. What are you?

JANE   I'm a dependent.

AUNT REED	And where are your parents?
JANE	*(Quietly)* Dead.
AUNT REED	What was that?
JANE	Dead.
AUNT REED	Did they leave you any money?
JANE	No.
AUNT REED	Without the situation you find yourself in, what would you be?

JANE hesitates, then:

JANE	An outcast and a beggar.
AUNT REED	An outcast and a beggar, that's right; not living in a place such as Gateshead Hall, eating fine meals, wearing fine clothes, all at my expense, and with honest, decent children to play with.
JANE	He's not honest!
AUNT REED	*(Harshly)* Do *not* speak out of turn, girl!

AUNT REED regains her composure. Her voice is controlled again.

> I warned my husband not to take you in, and it was the death of him. I wanted little enough to do with you, even at two years old. I have children of my own to raise. Yet here you live, in what...?

| JANE | Warmth and comfort. |

| AUNT REED | And what do we say? |

| JANE | *(Conditioned response)* Thank you, Aunt Reed. |

AUNT REED nods.

| AUNT REED | Now offer a hand of apology to John. |

From behind AUNT REED's back, JOHN REED says:

| REED | Apologise to me. *(Quieter)* Rat. |

JANE roars and launches herself at JOHN REED. He backs off, AUNT REED and GEORGIANA catch hold of her. JANE bucks and fights hard.

| GEORGIANA | Mama, she's too strong! |

| JOHN REED | She means to kill me! |

| AUNT REED | *(Calling)* Bessie! *Bessie!* Take this unruly thing to the Red Room! |

Music. JANE screams "No! No!" as JOHN REED laughs. AUNT REED and GEORGIANA turn JANE around as she bucks and screams. They lower JANE to her knees. JOHN REED joins them.

| JANE | Please! Don't leave me in here! Please! I'll say anything you want! I'll say I'm sorry! Please! |

There is the echoing sound of a door locking.

(Terrified; screaming) No...!

Oppressive, sinister music plays. We hear voices and see movement; a sequence reflecting the horror in JANE's mind, reaching a crescendo. Suddenly lights are brought up full and the music snaps out. Chairs have been drawn into the space. AUNT REED sits on one, TWO (as BROCKLEHURST) another and JANE stands in front of a third, head slightly bowed as the adults silently observe her; then:

BROCKLEHURST   She's a dour looking thing for sure.

AUNT REED   She is.

BROCKLEHURST   A relative of your late husband, you say?

AUNT REED   The mother was my husband's sister.

AUNT REED looks at JANE.

> He made the promise, Mr. Brocklehurst; not I.

BROCKLEHURST   She has the Devil in her; that much is clear.

AUNT REED   The trouble she has given me. God knows I've offered her every comfort; treated her as my own.

BROCKLEHURST   Hmmmm...

He stands.

> *(To JANE)* Do you not speak?

JANE   When spoken to, sir.

AUNT REED   See how truthfully she presents herself? I've kept my own children away from her as best I can, but... I think it's time.

BROCKLEHURST nods. He takes a step towards JANE.

BROCKLEHURST   Do you know who I am, child?

JANE   No, sir.

BROCKLEHURST   I run a charity school not far from here; a school your Aunt has applied to on your behalf.

A beat.

Education is a shining jewel; it has the power to elevate and enlighten. I should warn you however, deceit and wickedness have no place at Lowood. Do you understand?

JANE offers the most cursory of nods.

Would you consider yourself a good child?

JANE offers no reply.

Do you know where the wicked go after death?

JANE   They go to hell.

BROCKLEHURST   And what is hell?

JANE   A pit of fire.

BROCKLEHURST Would you like to fall into that pit and burn for evermore?

JANE No, sir.

BROCKLEHURST What must you do to avoid it?

JANE I must keep in good health and not die.

AUNT REED sighs audibly. A beat.

BROCKLEHURST Do you read your bible?

JANE Sometimes.

AUNT REED adjusts her position. Inside she is fuming.

BROCKLEHURST And do you know your Psalms?

JANE In part.

BROCKLEHURST "In part?"

JANE I find them uninteresting.

BROCKLEHURST I can see how you've tested your poor aunt.

With a look at AUNT REED, BROCKLEHURST quotes from the bible.

Revelations. *(Quoting)* "Here is a call for the endurance of the saints."

AUNT REED smiles. JANE completes the quote, staring fixedly at AUNT REED.

JANE   *(Quoting)* "Those who keep the commandments of God and their faith in Jesus."

A beat. AUNT REED controls her anger.

AUNT REED   Mr. Brocklehurst, if you do accept Jane Eyre, please instruct your teachers to keep the strictest eye on her. *(Looking at JANE)* Spare not the rod.

BROCKLEHURST Never. I shall inform Miss Temple to expect a new girl.

AUNT REED   Teach her as best you can... and keep her humble. As for the holidays, she will spend them always at Lowood.

BROCKLEHURST As you wish. Madam.

BROCKLEHURST exits. AUNT REED looks at JANE.

AUNT REED   I expect you think me cruel.

JANE says nothing.

This is the best course for all parties. I believe with time you will put your lies and deceit behind you. Until then I shall have to make do with a little gratitude. Now. What do we say?

JANE knows she is expected to thank her aunt but will not do it. AUNT REED is frustrated at her niece's lack of gratitude or understanding.

(Annoyed) Return to the nursery.

JANE turns to exit, pauses, then turns back.

JANE   I do not lie.

AUNT REED   I beg your pardon?

JANE   I do not lie. If I did, I'd tell you that I loved you, but I don't. I dislike you most of anyone in the world except John Reed. As for Georgiana, if you believe Lowood School rids people of deceitfulness then perhaps she should go in my place.

A beat.

AUNT REED   Have you finished?

JANE   No! I'm glad you're no relation of mine. I'll never call you aunt again as long as I live. You didn't need to tell Mr. Brocklehurst to keep me back during the holidays – nothing could make me return here willingly. I'll never come to see you when I leave, and if anyone asks me about you I'll say the thought of you, and the way you treated me, makes me sick.

AUNT REED   How *dare* you?

JANE   I'll remember you forcing me into the Red Room until the day I die. You punished me for your son's violent temper; I did nothing. It must suit you to think I deserve no better.

AUNT REED	You do not speak to your – *(elders in this way)*
JANE	People think you a good woman. What good woman would wish a child dead? *You're* the liar, Mrs. Reed, and the only comfort I take is that God in heaven can see you for what you truly are. So can my parents... and so can Uncle Reed.

Pause. AUNT REED is too stunned to speak. Slowly she stands and leaves the room. JANE addresses the audience.

> *(To audience)* That victory... that realisation that I had a voice – was the spur for all that followed, though I hadn't found the desire to channel it just yet. Of my early life at Gateshead Hall, you have seen all I wish to show you. Now comes Lowood School; both the good... and the bad.

The company assemble and sing a rousing version of the song Bessie sings to JANE in the novel (Poor Orphan Child) as we see something of JANE's journey to Lowood.

COMPANY

My feet they are sore and my limbs they are weary
Long is the way, and the mountains are wild;
Soon will the twilight close moonless and dreary
Over the path of the poor orphan child.

Why did they send me so far and so lonely
Up where the moors spread and grey rocks are piled?

Men are hard-hearted, and kind angels only
Watch o'er the steps of a poor orphan child.

The song accompanies a reconfiguring of the space. JANE takes a slate from the pile of burnt-looking things, a piece of chalk from a pocket and begins to write. THREE and FOUR sit on the other chairs with their own slates and write too. Music underscores. JANE addresses the audience, quietly; almost conspiratorially.

JANE *(To audience)* Three weeks later. A murky February day.

JANE stops as THREE looks across at her, only continuing once THREE has turned back to her slate.

Lowood School is much as I'd imagined it would be. It has dark bricks, high walls and eighty girls within. I enjoy the lessons, though of the teachers only Miss Temple could be described as kind. Mr. Brocklehurst's visits are few... though not few enough...

The music stops as BROCKLEHURST enters.

BROCKLEHURST Good morning school.

JANE, THREE and FOUR stand and intone:

ALL Good morning Mr. Brocklehurst; good morning all.

In standing, JANE has dropped her slate.

BROCKLEHURST Remain standing, that girl!

JANE stands nervously as THREE and FOUR sit; their heads down.

Ah! The new pupil. Craving undue attention, no doubt. Step forward Jane Eyre, and climb on that chair. Let all see you.

She climbs on a chair facing out so the audience can see her reaction to his words.

School, this child was sent to me by her benefactress, a most pious and trustworthy lady who she saw fit to deceive, as Satan's will took her. Be in no doubt, ladies – Jane Eyre is a *liar*.

Gasps and murmurs.

Lies are the Devil speaking through us, are they not?

The other actors answer as a chorus.

CHORUS   Yes Mr. Brocklehurst.

BROCKLEHURST Proverbs. *(Quoting)* "Lying lips are an abomination to the Lord, but those who act faithfully are his delight."

CHORUS   Yes Mr. Brocklehurst.

BROCKLEHURST Miss Scatcherd? See to it that Jane Eyre stands on this chair a full hour more. She is to be left alone; no girl may look at her nor speak to her. Teachers? Take your forms back to their classrooms. *(As he is leaving)* Good morning, school.

CHORUS   Good morning Mr. Brocklehurst.

BROCKLEHURST exits. Music. THREE and FOUR exit also.

JANE   *(To audience)* Alone I stood at the end of the cold hall, shivering and broken. The day had started with praise for both my grammar and my French... now all was undone. Who would want to associate herself with someone as damned as I had been?

FOUR enters quietly. She is now HELEN Burns, an ailing, older child. She turns and looks at JANE. She hastily writes something on her slate, then approaches JANE surreptitiously. She holds the slate up for JANE to read. On it is written one word. "Hello." JANE looks round, then looks back at HELEN, who is smiling. JANE offers a small wave by way of a response. HELEN nods, erases "Hello" and writes, "Hungry?" JANE nods. HELEN looks at her sympathetically then reaches into her pocket and pulls out a small piece of bread. She offers it to JANE who resolutely shakes her head. HELEN frowns and offers it again. Once again JANE shakes her head but she is clearly hungry. She points at HELEN as much as to say "It's yours." HELEN shakes her head. JANE nods.

HELEN   Take it.

JANE inhales with shock, then looks around in case she's been heard.

JANE	You mustn't talk to me. Miss Scatcherd will punish you.
HELEN	Nothing new there. Eat.

JANE takes the bread. She smiles at HELEN. HELEN returns the smile then coughs, covering her mouth with a handkerchief. She wipes her mouth and says:

I'm Helen.

JANE smiles and nods.

I know who you are. *(Imitating BROCKLEHURST)* "The wicked child."

JANE smiles again, then remembers her situation.

JANE	Why would you talk to me?
HELEN	Why not?
JANE	Everyone here thinks I'm a liar.
HELEN	I'm sure they don't.
JANE	They'll despise me.
HELEN	Pity you more like.
JANE	After what Mr. Brocklehurst said?
HELEN	He's not God, you know. He's not even that well liked. Far better that he made an example of you than showed you favour. Many here have been where you are now.
JANE	You?

HELEN	Several times. "Burns, you are untidy." Or, "Burns, you are late." "Burns, you are avoiding lessons."

JANE joins in.

JANE	*(Imitating BROCKLEHURST)* "Burns, you are talking to a child on a chair."
HELEN	"A lying child."
JANE	"A forbidden child."

JANE is now beaming. HELEN smiles too.

HELEN	Eat. Go on.

JANE takes a small bite.

> Be true to yourself, Jane. Even if you feel the whole world hates you, your conscience and your pure soul will keep you in God's love.

THREE enters clutching books and wearing a pince-nez. She is now Miss TEMPLE, a good-hearted teacher with a worried expression on her face.

TEMPLE	Helen Burns! Here you are!

At this, both JANE and HELEN start. TEMPLE approaches.

HELEN	Here I am, Miss Temple.

TEMPLE looks at JANE, then back to HELEN.

TEMPLE	I see you have broken the rules.

43

A beat, then a smile creeps onto her face.

> *(To JANE)* I think that's long enough up there, don't you? Come on.

TEMPLE holds a hand out for JANE to step down. JANE takes it.

> Sit a moment. Rest yourself.

She leads JANE to the row of seats. JANE sits where she sat previously; HELEN sits by her side. TEMPLE crouches before JANE.

> I know what you did today was an accident. And I can see in your eyes that this is not the first injustice done you, so I will make you this promise. I will clear you of all wrong in the eyes of the school... if —

TEMPLE holds for a moment to build tension. JANE looks nervous.

> — you join Helen and I in my chambers tonight and tell your sorry tale.

A beat.

> There'll be bread and butter, and seed-cake.

JANE nods.

> *(To HELEN)* Will you show her the way?

HELEN   Yes.

She coughs again.

TEMPLE   Then it's settled. Come on, Helen; it's time
for your rest. Until later, Jane.

*TEMPLE stands. The pupils do likewise. She exits. HELEN
and JANE look at one another, then JANE throws her arms
around HELEN and hugs her tight. HELEN kisses her on the
cheek and exits. Music. JANE addresses the audience.*

JANE   *(To audience)* The next day, after
listening to stories of Aunt Reed, John and
Georgiana – and of the Red Room – Miss
Temple addressed the whole school,
attesting to my honesty. That pardon
brought me companions with whom to
play; gave me the confidence to learn...
and brought Helen and I together.

HELEN crosses the stage, her nose in a book.

(To HELEN) What's that?

HELEN   *Rasselas.* Samuel Johnson. *(Shutting the
book)* Which I've just finished.

JANE   *(Wide-eyed)* You've read so many books!

HELEN   *(Wide-eyed; gently teasing)* And you've
jumped so many fences!

*HELEN has to stop to cough. JANE looks concerned, but when
the fit subsides, HELEN pulls a silly face at JANE and they
smile.*

Come on. I know what I want to read next!

HELEN moves to the doorway. JANE watches her go.

JANE   *(To audience)* That winter and spring
when I was ten I recognise now as my first
taste of happiness. But just like sun
breaking briefly through clouds on a
stormy day, happiness can be fleeting.
May turned...

*Music. HELEN coughs, and her breathing is suddenly more
laboured.*

...and brought with it typhus.

*THREE enters, also coughing. Then TWO, FIVE and FOUR.
All cough softly as they reconfigure the space.*

It tore through Lowood School like a
hurricane wind, taking forty-five souls to
the hereafter... Helen was shut up
somewhere in one of the rooms on the
second floor. She was spared typhus... but
not her end. She was consumptive.

*TEMPLE lowers HELEN to the floor, where she sits shivering in
front of a flickering birdie lamp. Her breathing is now ragged and
shallow. TEMPLE places a blanket around her before exiting.*

The last night I spent with her was in front
of the fire in Miss Temple's chambers.
Stealing past teachers and physicians
alike, I ran to her side like I had never run
before...

JANE turns into the scene. She is out of breath. HELEN looks at her and smiles. Music subsides.

HELEN   You... sound worse... than me.

JANE throws herself at HELEN, holding her; smothering her with kisses.

JANE   They didn't tell me... they kept... kept me away...

HELEN   Stop... stop. It's all right.

HELEN wipes JANE's face with a weak hand.

                   Who let you up here?

JANE   No-one.

HELEN smiles.

HELEN   *(Weak impersonation of Brocklehurst)* "Always the rule-breaker, Jane Eyre. I ought... to make you stand on the chair..."

She laughs again before descending into a coughing fit.

                   I hoped to see you. Dearly. Now we can say good-bye.

JANE   Are you going somewhere else?

The naivety of this makes HELEN laugh, which, in turn, makes JANE laugh through the fear of loss. HELEN looks at JANE.

HELEN   I am going... to my last home.

JANE	No!
HELEN	Don't grieve, Jane. We all die, and I'm not in pain. My mind's at rest. I am going... going to God.
JANE	But what if there's nothing? How do you know it's all real?
HELEN	I have faith. In God the Father, and in heaven above.
JANE	And will I see you again when I...
HELEN	No doubt. Dear Jane. Dear... dear...

A coughing fit consumes HELEN momentarily, after which:

Oh! That last fit's tired me out. I think I could sleep a little. Would you stay with me? Here, by the fire?

JANE   No-one will take me away.

HELEN opens the blanket and JANE snuggles inside it. HELEN puts her head onto JANE's shoulder.

HELEN   Will you sleep?

JANE   Yes.

They look at one another for a moment.

HELEN   Good-night, Jane.

JANE   Good-night, Helen.

They kiss, then close their eyes. Music swells. A movement piece, at once beautiful and sad, takes HELEN off. The stage is reconfigured. The other members of the company divest JANE of the trappings of childhood (mop-cap perhaps; something youthful) and bring her a pair of cases. When the movement sequence finishes we see THREE enter as FAIRFAX. Music subsides.

FAIRFAX   Miss Eyre, is it?

JANE   *(To audience)* It's eight years later.

FAIRFAX   Jane? Jane Eyre?

JANE   That's right.

FAIRFAX   Mary said she'd shown you in. *(Calling off)* Mary? *(To JANE)* I thought she'd have popped you in my sitting room at least. *(Calling off)* Mary! *(To JANE)* Sorry about this...

She exits momentarily.

JANE   *(To audience)* I'm standing in the kitchen office at Thornfield Hall. It's a crisp afternoon in September and I'm preparing to start the next part of my life...

FAIRFAX returns.

FAIRFAX   Hasn't the sense she was born with. No matter. I'm Mrs. Fairfax.

JANE   I got your letter.

FAIRFAX   Course you did; course you did. Welcome to Thornfield.

They shake hands.

> Dear me; your hand's like ice. Get yourself closer to the fire.

JANE   Thank you.

JANE adjusts her chair. There is a slightly awkward pause. She and FAIRFAX smile at one another. JANE attempts to make conversation.

> The pictures along the passage... are...

FAIRFAX   ...stern looking men standing by windows? Yes. Never been keen personally. Still, they've been up so long I barely see them. Now. Let's get to it. What made you advertise your services?

JANE   Oh; I'd... taught for two years and... it just felt like the right time for a change. Or a challenge.

FAIRFAX   I daresay you'll get both.

JANE   And, well, a governess position seemed...

JANE is momentarily lost for words. FAIRFAX smiles kindly.

> Will I meet Miss Fairfax this evening?

FAIRFAX   Miss Fairfax?

JANE   Yes; I – is it not your daughter I'm attending to?

FAIRFAX	Mine? She's not mine. Heaven forbid. No; you're here for Miss *Varens*. *(Conspiratorially)* She's French.
JANE	I see.
FAIRFAX	We'll spare you that pleasure until the morning; let you get a feel for the house.
JANE	And will I meet *Mr.* Fairfax this evening?
FAIRFAX	I hope not; he's been dead eight years. You wouldn't want him floating about. Mind, I hardly liked it any better when he was alive.
JANE	I thought... with you replying to my advertisement...
FAIRFAX	*(Laughing)* Give over; I'm just the housekeeper. The master here is Mr. Rochester, but he's not in residence at the moment; he travels. Now, I'll show you around, then you can get yourself settled for the evening.

She tinkles a hand bell. JANE picks up one of her cases and prepares to take another.

> William'll see to that. I've put you in one of the rooms at the back – not as grand as the ones out front but cosier.

FIVE comes forward as WILLIAM.

William, take Miss Eyre's luggage up, will
you?

WILLIAM nods and takes the cases.

JANE   Nice to meet you...

WILLIAM hurries through a doorway and exits.

FAIRFAX   Oh, you'll get nothing out of William until
he's known you a month, and that'll be
less than a grunt. The master's very
particular about how we do things here; he
won't want you speaking to the servants
as if they're equals. They're in one part of
the house, we're in another – and never the
twain shall meet.

*They take a definite step together. FAIRFAX gestures to indicate
a door.*

This is the library. It's pretty well stocked
I'm told; though I'm more of a tatter than
a reader. Do you tat?

JANE   I read.

FAIRFAX   Hmmmm. You'll teach in the library most
days; I'll trust you to set your own hours.
Shall we?

*FAIRFAX moves off. JANE follows, looking around. Music –
a physical sequence; the other cast members moving boxes and
chairs to provide obstacles, things to step up and so on so as to make
the journey round the house interesting. FAIRFAX traverses these*

obstacles with ease, talking as she goes. JANE less so. They stop
for a moment.

> This is Mr. Rochester's study. We don't go
> in when he's in residence. We don't go in
> when he's not. Hasn't been dusted in years
> to my knowledge; I dread to think what's
> lurking about in there. Follow me.

More music, more movement.

> Adèle's room's on the left just here.
> Nursery's back that way. Master's
> chamber just round the corner there... and
> here...

FAIRFAX turns JANE around.

> ...is your room.

WILLIAM enters with the cases. He can barely catch his breath;
he is exhausted.

> Thank you, William. That'll be all.

She dismisses him. He looks at her and exits. Laughter
(BERTHA). FAIRFAX doesn't react at all.

JANE   What was that?

FAIRFAX   What was what?

JANE   Sounded like laughter – from the floor
                  above, perhaps?

FAIRFAX   Oh. Yes. Should have mentioned that.
                  Don't go up there. It's not in the best of

53

order – the ceiling above the gallery could come in any day. Master knows about it... and Grace, of course. That's who you'll have heard.

JANE Who?

FAIRFAX One of the servants. Grace Poole. You'll hear her scuttling about from time to time – mind, that's with you being new. It'll just become like any other noise eventually; I hardly hear it.

JANE smiles. A beat.

I'll leave you to it then. Unless you want to join me in my sitting room? I could teach you to tat.

JANE I think I'll... I think I'll read.

FAIRFAX Each to their own. Breakfast's at seven sharp.

FAIRFAX moves upstage, joining the others. They watch JANE. She sits and looks around her. The sound of laughter echoes faintly. Music swells

Meanwhile TWO and FIVE move furniture to create another space; a library. FOUR enters holding a bride puppet. She is ADELE. She sits the puppet on JANE's knee before performing a little dance. FAIRFAX stands behind JANE, both watching the young child cavort. She completes the dance with a flourish. JANE and FAIRFAX applaud politely. TWO and FIVE exit. ADELE bows low.

JANE	*(To ADELE)* Ah! Mais tu danse! C'est merveilleuse.
ADELE	*(Delighted)* Merci mademoiselle! Merci!
JANE	Et ton anglais parlant?
ADELE	Non; je n'aime que danser. Encore une fois, oui?
FAIRFAX	Oh! That means "again." The master taught me that one.
JANE	Thank you Mrs. Fairfax. *(To ADELE)* On peut danser plus tard. Etudie d'abord.

ADELE huffs.

ADELE	*(Faltering)* I like dance.
JANE	You like *to* dance.
ADELE	*To* dance.
JANE	That much is clear.
FAIRFAX	*(Under her breath)* It's all she bloody does.

JANE looks at FAIRFAX.

You'll see.

JANE stands; the puppet slips from her lap. ADELE is horrified and snatches it up.

ADELE	Oh! Therese! Vous l'avez laissée tomber!

She nurses her puppet tenderly and pouts at JANE. FAIRFAX rolls her eyes.

JANE	I promise we shall dance, little one.

ADELE struggles to follow but on hearing the word dance her eyes light up.

	We shall also draw, and play the piano. In between, we shall learn English, mathematics, history, geography...
FAIRFAX	Good luck with that.
JANE	*(Ignoring FAIRFAX)* And you shall teach me about this house.
ADELE	C'est comment?
JANE	I want to hear about its history – as far as you know it; its mysterious master... and any strange stories you might have.

A stream of complex French follows, ADELE protesting about the amount of things she doesn't understand, over which FAIRFAX is telling JANE that the girl knows nothing about the house and the master would think it best that she best stick to the subjects for which she was appointed. After a moment or two of this, JANE stands.

> Ladies, please!

Both ADELE and FAIRFAX calm down.

> To begin: Adèle, do you know the days of the week?

ADELE looks confused.

> Les jours de la semaine.

ADELE   Ah... *(faltering)* Monday... Tuesday...
                 Thursday... Wednesday... Friday...
                 Sunday... Saturday.

JANE   Right names, wrong order.

FAIRFAX   *(Lively)* Encore une fois!

                 A beat. JANE looks at her.

                 Sorry. Carry on. Sorry.

*Music. A sequence. ADELE walks her puppet offstage. JANE
addresses the audience as the stage is
reconfigured by FAIRFAX, TWO and
FIVE (FIVE as WILLIAM)
Occasionally they might push wheelbarrows
containing plants or gardening equipment, or
carry barrels past to indicate time moving on.
ADELE dances around them, sporadically
offering English phrases.*

JANE   *(To audience)* And so my new life began at
                 Thornfield Hall. Adèle was a lively
                 student; desperate for praise and willing to
                 work to get it... when she wasn't dancing.

ADELE dances past.

ADELE   Monday, Tuesday, Wednesday, Thursday,
                 Friday... Saturday Sunday!

JANE   *(To audience)* The house didn't have as
                 large a staff as Gateshead, but those there
                 were worked twice as hard.

FAIRFAX	We never know when the master might return, Jane. We have to keep things in order.
ADELE	One for sorrow, two for joy, three for a girl and four for a boy…
JANE	*(To audience)* The grounds were wide, lush and well-attended, and the views from my window magnificent. I made time to sit and sketch there as often as I could.
WILLIAM	Cold's coming in.
FAIRFAX	You'll feel it less if you worked harder. Get moving!
JANE	*(To audience)* The burning fires of autumn gave way to the frosts of winter. Still I taught; still Adèle danced, still Mrs. Fairfax tried to get me to tat…
FAIRFAX	We could try a little crochet tonight if you fancy.
JANE	*(To audience)* I didn't fancy.
ADELE	The brown dog is under the table. He is a friendly dog.
JANE	Good, Adèle! Bien!

ADELE beams and dances away, doll in hand.

	(To audience) I had gotten to know the maids and grooms and cook and stable

boys by name. The laughing Grace Poole alone eluded me.

FAIRFAX   Pay her no mind, Jane. She's a shy, troubled girl. Now; see – the Christmas trees are here!

JANE   *(To audience)* Dressed for Christmas, Thornfield looked nothing short of spectacular.

ADELE   We play piano later, yes? I have been practicing.

FAIRFAX   Don't we know it. 'Encore une bloody fois' indeed. Come on.

ADELE and FAIRFAX exit. JANE is alone on stage.

JANE   *(To audience)* As the weeks rolled on my restless spirit, at first kept in check by the novelty of life as a governess, was beginning to stir. Wanting more than Lowood had spurred me to seek this position, and though there was beauty and comfort here I couldn't help but think I had swapped one routine for another. Is this all I was to amount to?

Music ends. WILLIAM walks across the stage carrying a sack of potatoes over his shoulder.

WILLIAM   I wouldn't be out here too much longer, Miss. Chilly tonight.

JANE	No, of course. I'll be in presently. Thank you, William.
WILLIAM	Merry Christmas, Miss.
JANE	Merry Christmas.

WILLIAM exits.

(To audience) The year turned with neither sight nor sound of the mysterious Mr. Rochester. And I believe that had winter progressed into spring with no further change from day to day I might have sought a situation elsewhere. Then, one frosty afternoon in mid-January, Mrs. Fairfax sought me out in the grounds; asked me if I would –

FAIRFAX enters.

FAIRFAX   Take a letter to the Post Office in Hay.

She hands JANE a letter and exits. Music resumes. Lights change.

JANE   *(To audience)* It was my first chance to explore the world beyond Thornfield. Following the road to the first sign post, I discerned Hay's direction and headed away from the beaten track, first walking on little-used footpaths and ultimately entering a small copse...

She begins to sing the "Poor Orphan Child" song – firstly to herself, then accompanied:

> My feet they are sore and my limbs they
> are weary,
> Long is the way and the mountains are
> wild;
> Soon will the twilight close moonless and
> dreary
> O'er the path of the poor... orphan...
> child...

Through the music we hear the rhythmic thump of a drum. JANE looks scared – we hear the barking of a dog, the pounding of hooves... then JANE lifts up her arms as if to protect herself. There is the scream of a horse in pain. ROCHESTER enters, as if he has been thrown.

> Are you injured, sir?

ROCHESTER   Pilot! Shut up!

JANE backs away.

> Shut up, damn you!

ROCHESTER thrashes out. PILOT whines. ROCHESTER stands with difficulty.

JANE   Can I help you?

ROCHESTER looks at JANE.

ROCHESTER   Stand to one side. The horse won't settle with you there to hex her.

With a grunt he stands.

Where are you headed?

JANE   *(Surprised by the question)* To Hay, sir. I've a letter to post.

ROCHESTER   Don't let me stop you.

He puts weight on his ankle. Winces.

Well? On, elf; your mischief is made.

JANE   I'm no elf, and I won't leave until I know you're well enough to move.

ROCHESTER is silent; staring at JANE intently.

I can go on to Hay to fetch help if you wish, or... or back to Thornfield; I believe the – *(housekeeper might be able to bind your ankle)*

ROCHESTER   Thornfield Hall?

JANE   Yes sir.

ROCHESTER   How do you know the place?

JANE   I'm the governess there.

ROCHESTER   Really?

JANE nods her head.

And the master of the house there would be...?

JANE   His name is Rochester, though if you were intent on visiting him, I'm afraid he's away.

ROCHESTER takes a step towards JANE. Looks her over.

ROCHESTER   There'll be no need for further assistance. You can help me yourself. Lead her to me.

JANE hesitates. ROCHESTER softens his voice with effort.

If you please.

JANE moves as though approaching a horse. We hear the sound of it snuffling, snorting, and scuffing its hooves. Images onscreen to accompany the action.

Take hold of the bridle.

JANE reaches out tentatively but recoils when the horse whinnies.

Come here.

She goes to him. He leans heavily on her. They move a few steps together.

That's close enough; she'll follow me now.

A beat.

Thank you. Now, make haste to Hay with your letter and return as fast as you can. The sky darkens even now. Pilot!

ROCHESTER exits. Music.

JANE   *(To audience)* I watched the stranger lurch on awkwardly; every step seeming to pain him. The encounter, I considered as I descended into Hay, was an exciting colour to add to the day's adventure. Returning at dusk to Thornfield's familiar palette made my heart sink. Then...

ADELE dashes up to JANE.

ADELE   Ah; mademoiselle! Il est enfin revenu! Venez! Venez!

JANE   Qu'est-ce que se passe ici? Il faut dormir.

ADELE   Non! Non!

She calms herself down and says in her best English:

The Master has come home. He's here.

ADELE shrieks with delight.

JANE   Calme-toi; calme-toi.

ADELE   He is in the... library? Yes. Come with me!

She takes JANE by the hand and they dash off. Music. A quick change on stage. Lights. JANE and ADELE enter.

Non! He was here!

FAIRFAX   Aye; he was. He went to his study. He'll be back before you know it.

ADELE   But I do know it!

FAIRFAX   It's a figure of speech, you cheeky bloody article.

ROCHESTER appears in the doorway, temporarily walking with the aid of a cane. He carries JANE's letters of application. He walks past JANE and sits.

ADELE   Monsieur; voici ma gouvernante!

ROCHESTER   Unhand your "gouvernante" then; let her sit. If she is willing.

JANE remains standing. ROCHESTER regards her.

FAIRFAX   Mr. Rochester, this is Jane Eyre. A fine addition to the household and a wonderful governess.

ROCHESTER   Don't trouble yourself to give her character; I'll judge for myself.

FAIRFAX   Jane, this is Mr. Edward Fairfax Rochester. We're distant relations, you see; on my husband's side...

A beat.

I'll make some tea.

FAIRFAX exits.

ADELE   Monsieur; est-ce que vous avez un cadeau pour moi?

ROCHESTER   Who talks of "cadeaux?"

ADELE   *(To JANE; doing her best)* When the master come back from his travels –

JANE   *(Softly) Comes* back.

ADELE   …from his travels he brings… me always gifts. Perhaps you too.

ROCHESTER   *(To ADELE)* Why? Is she expecting "un cadeau" as well?

ADELE doesn't know how to answer. She looks to JANE.

                       (To JANE) Do you like gifts, Miss Eyre?

JANE   Most people think them pleasant.

ROCHESTER   I'm not talking to most people; I'm talking to you.

JANE   I have little experience of them.

ADELE   Monsieur… *(mes cadeaux…?)*

ROCHESTER   *(Pointing)* La bas.

ADELE goes to investigate.

ROCHESTER   *(To JANE)* Sit down.

JANE sits. ROCHESTER looks at ADELE; then:

                       You've taken pains with her. She's not bright and has no talents but you've improved her; I can see that.

JANE is shocked that ROCHESTER would say this in front of ADELE but tries her best to hide it. ADELE rushes forward with a soldier puppet.

ADELE   Un soldat! Merci, monsieur!

She turns to JANE.

C'est quoi, *soldat?*

JANE   Soldier.

ADELE   Soldier! And now he can marry Therese and there will be love here in Thornfield! *(To ROCHESTER)* Merci, merci, merci!

She kisses a resisting ROCHESTER.

This is how mama say thank you, yes?

ROCHESTER   Precisely... and charmed my English gold out of my British pockets. Off now and show Mrs. Fairfax.

ADELE curtseys and runs off.

ADELE   *(Calling to FAIRFAX)* Madame!

She exits. Pause.

ROCHESTER   Doubtless you have questions.

JANE smiles politely and shakes her head.

Very well.

ROCHESTER looks at JANE's letters of recommendation

(Reading) Eight years at Lowood School... six as a pupil, two as teacher... a glowing reference from a Mrs. Naysmith, nee Temple. Former colleague...?

JANE   Yes sir.

ROCHESTER   No mention of any family.

JANE	I have none.
ROCHESTER	Ah! The Tragic Cliché of the Lonely Governess.

JANE says nothing.

> Do you play?

JANE	Play?
ROCHESTER	Or were you not taught at Lowood?

He gestures to the piano.

JANE	A little, sir.
ROCHESTER	I sense a conditioned response. I want evidence.
JANE	Now?
ROCHESTER	The sooner the better.

JANE moves to the piano, sits and plays a short piece, until:

> Enough!

A beat. JANE stands.

> You were quite right. You play a *little*. Return. Sit.

She moves back to the chair.

> Well? Speak!

JANE looks at ROCHESTER.

You are annoyed.

She remains fixed on him.

No? Stubborn then.

Still nothing.

Miss Eyre, life has dealt me blows, and when struck, one tends to strike back. Now, despite your attempts to bewitch my horse earlier I find myself in gregarious mood... that will not last. I have no time for the prattle of children or the ramblings of old ladies, so it falls to you to divert my thoughts – and quick; before my tempers are irreparably changed.

A beat. ROCHESTER sighs.

It's not my desire to treat you like an inferior. The only superiority I claim over you is that of age. Now, might you consent to a little conversation... and some mild hectoring... on those terms?

JANE   Few masters would trouble to ask their paid subordinates that.

ROCHESTER   Paid? Ah; the salary! Of course. On that mercenary ground then.

JANE   Not on *that* ground, no.

ROCHESTER   *(Amused)* Intriguing.

JANE	I can't start a conversation without knowing what amuses you. Better that you ask me questions; I'll do my best to answer them.
ROCHESTER	That's evasive.
JANE	It's polite.
ROCHESTER	*(Amused)* Ha!

A beat.

> I have gotten quite out of the habit of fencing in this way. So... you *will* converse, in the manner you suggest... but *not* because I pay you.

JANE nods.

> Then why?

JANE	Because you had forgotten about the salary when you asked. And because you care whether or not a dependant is comfortable in his dependency.
ROCHESTER	I care, do I?
JANE	Yes, sir.
ROCHESTER	Mmm. And setting superiority aside, will you agree to receive orders now and then, without being piqued by the tone of command?
JANE	I believe I will. Now I know you.

A beat. ROCHESTER looks at her. She doesn't hide from his gaze.

ROCHESTER   Do you find me handsome?

JANE   No.

ROCHESTER barks out another laugh.

    Forgive me.

ROCHESTER   Certainly not.

JANE   I should've said... tastes differ; beauty is of little consequence... or something of that nature.

ROCHESTER   "Something of that nature?"

JANE   Please; allow me to disown my response.

ROCHESTER   Never! Now, once you have finished searching the carpet with your eyes, tell me what faults you find with me?

JANE   I didn't mean to offend you.

ROCHESTER   There's no offence.

JANE looks at ROCHESTER.

    Your honesty is remarkable. I applaud you for it. And though you're no prettier than I am handsome I'd wager not three in three thousand governesses would have spoken with me as you have this evening; paid subordinates or not.

71

A beat.

> I've enjoyed our first meeting, Miss Eyre. Badinage is sorely lacking here. Perhaps next time we shall find ourselves a spot more suited to private conversation.

JANE stands.

> Where are you going?

JANE   To put Adèle to bed; it's late.

ROCHESTER stands and approaches her.

ROCHESTER   You're afraid of me.

JANE shakes her head ever so slightly.

> Bewildered then.

JANE   I don't wish to talk nonsense.

ROCHESTER   I'm sure if you did I'd mistake it for sense.

On the verge of a response, JANE checks herself and simply offers:

JANE   Goodnight, sir.

ROCHESTER laughs.

ROCHESTER   Do you never laugh, Miss Eyre?

He shakes his head.

> You really are a solemn creature.

He exits. JANE turns to the audience. Behind her the stage is reconfigured slightly; the chairs being moved by FIVE and THREE. FOUR plays something to underscore.

JANE   *(To audience)* He was changeful and abrupt, appearing on first evidence to think a great deal of himself... and he'd mocked my past mercilessly, yet hinted of the troubles within him too. I wondered if he might reveal to me what those troubles were. As it turned out, I did not have to wait too long...

JANE moves to a different part of the stage – this is now ROCHESTER's study. ROCHESTER enters holding a candle and a number of JANE's sketches.

ROCHESTER   What do you think of my study?

JANE   Very...

She notices her sketches.

Where did you get those?

ROCHESTER   I found them scattered across the nursery floor, with crude copies lying next to them. In crayon.

JANE   *(Smiling)* I see.

ROCHESTER   Where did *you* copy them from?

JANE   Nowhere!

ROCHESTER   Ah! That pricks pride.

He looks at them again as he speaks.

Home almost two months and only now am I discovering this talent?

JANE   I hid it from no-one.

ROCHESTER   That much is evident – Adèle's clearly a fan. Were you happy when you drew these?

JANE   Yes sir.

ROCHESTER   Really?

He looks at another.

I dread to imagine how *I* might appear in a Jane Eyre original. Are you satisfied with them?

JANE   Not at all.

ROCHESTER   *(Laughing)* What a mystery you are!

JANE   I mean to say... what I see far exceeds what I'm able to produce.

ROCHESTER gives JANE her sketches back. They sit.

ROCHESTER   You've been asking Mrs. Fairfax about me. Doubtless she's painted a grim portrait.

JANE   Not at all.

ROCHESTER	How was it? "His father and brother conspired against him all their lives; even at their deaths?"
JANE	No, sir.
ROCHESTER	"He's unsettled; won't stay at the house more than two weeks at a time?" Did she tell you about the Caribbean? Or... Adèle's mother! That'd be the topic. There's a fruit ripe enough for old Fairfax's appetite.
JANE	She talked in no great detail.
ROCHESTER	If you wish to know me, Miss Eyre, ask me yourself.

Pause.

Her name... was Céline. She performed at the Paris Opera House.

Music in background. FOUR (as CELINE) sings a piece of opera (Regret), which underscores (the translations for each line appear in italics below):

CELINE

Molto tempo fa ho desiderato andarmene
(A long time ago I wanted to leave)
"La casa in cui sono nato;"
("The house where I was born")
Molto tempo fa mi doleva
(A long time ago I was aching)
La mia casa sembrava cosi abbandonata

(My house seemed so abandoned)

As CELINE sings:

ROCHESTER I met her at a time when self-destruction had moved from hobby to mission. Held her high upon a pedestal. Lavished her with... well; anything. Hotel rooms, fine clothes, a position in Paris society. Made believe she was all mine. And she let me, of course. I was a means to an end. And that end... well.

A beat.

It's the first time I've spoken of this. I'm not even sure why I began.

JANE There was another?

A beat.

ROCHESTER A stripling. A whelp... when I found her with him she didn't even look surprised.

JANE doesn't answer.

I allowed him the courtesy of dressing before winging him with my pistol. Then, amid howling protestations of loneliness and regret, I ended the affair.

The singing stops.

She took the last money I'd given her and fled the city; abandoning Adèle. I don't know if she's mine – her mother said she was but I see no resemblance, and more days than enough I wish she wasn't. Still, I couldn't see an innocent child starving on the Paris streets, illegitimate or not.

JANE looks at ROCHESTER.

There. I wonder how you might paint me now you know the truth. Or Adèle, come to that.

JANE Adèle isn't answerable for her mother's faults. Or her father's.

A beat.

ROCHESTER I should... let you withdraw.

JANE stands. ROCHESTER hands her the lit candle on the table.

Thank you for allowing me to look at your pictures. Tomorrow I'll show you some drawings I obtained in Paris. See how the style compares to your own. If you'd like.

JANE nods. ROCHESTER exits. Music.

JANE *(To audience)* It was a freedom I'd never experienced; a voice I scarcely knew I had. His tone changed over time to one of easy cordiality, and though he drove our conversations, I was given ample opportunity to speak and found that no subject was off limits; everything was fair game for dissection and challenge. And...

...the face I had once described as less than handsome... was now the thing I best liked to see; his presence in a room more cheering than the brightest fire. He could be moody, and bitter; proud, too – but he could not hide his goodness beneath any of the hinted-at misdeeds.

I tried to find reasons why he might have lingered at Thornfield longer than he had in years; to temper my hopes... yet each night, as I read by my candle, I thrilled at the possibility that I might somehow be the cause.

Laughter. Music changes to something more sinister. JANE starts.

On Valentine's night the laughter rang out again; louder than I'd heard it in weeks, and with a growing malice...

Laughter once more, the volume raised.

It was no longer above me. It was close and getting closer. A creak on the stair near my door. I covered my candle and opened it; just a crack...

JANE moves into the space, her hand over the flame of the candle.

(Calling) Hello...?

We suddenly see THREE as BERTHA wearing a tattered bridal veil. There is a loud scream. BERTHA has gone and we're left with the confused and terrified JANE.

>Hello? Who's that?

A beat.

>Grace...?

The sounds of a fire kindling and growing.

>*(To audience)* The figure moved around the corner in the passage. I followed but it had gone. *(Calling)* Are you Grace? *(To audience)* I smelled the smoke, and followed it... to Mr. Rochester's door.

She coughs.

>*(Calling)* Sir? *(To audience)* Acrid, greasy smoke slipped under the door, scarcely hiding the flames within. *(Calling)* Mr. Rochester! *(To audience)* There was no time to think – I hurled myself at the door!

Music continues. We see ROCHESTER sitting in a chair, head bowed.

>*(Calling)* Wake up, sir! Wake up! *(To audience)* There on his night stand – his pitcher and basin. With the first I quenched the flames; the second I used to douse him utterly...

A physical sequence; JANE mimes throwing water over ROCHESTER, who is suddenly awake. Music fades.

ROCHESTER   Are you mad? Do you mean to drown me?

JANE   There's been a fire.

ROCHESTER   Is that Jane Eyre?

JANE   Yes sir.

He moves to her; takes her arms.

ROCHESTER   What have you done to me, witch? Sorceress?

JANE   Someone has plotted against you; I swear it wasn't me.

ROCHESTER   Plot? What's this talk of a plot?

JANE   There's someone here – someone...

They break from one another.

I heard... laughter; and – *(there was a presence)*

ROCHESTER   *(Quickly)* Did you see anyone?

JANE   Only a shadow, sir. I should call Mrs. Fairfax.

ROCHESTER   What for?

JANE   She could speak to her.

ROCHESTER   To who?

JANE   Grace Poole.

A beat. ROCHESTER looks at JANE.

               She's on your staff; she... I hear her
               laughing, and – *(yet I've not met her)*

ROCHESTER   Grace Poole. Yes. She'll not disturb us
                  further tonight. I'll deal with this myself.

A beat.

               You are no talking fool; might I ask that
               you keep what you have seen tonight to
               yourself?

JANE   Of course, sir.

ROCHESTER   Then return to your room. I shall explain
                  the state of mine in the morning.

A beat.

JANE   Very well, sir. Good night.

JANE turns to leave. ROCHESTER catches her arm.

ROCHESTER   You're leaving?

JANE nods.

               You've just saved me from an excruciating
               death! You shouldn't depart as if we're
               strangers. At least shake hands.

He holds out a hand. She puts hers in his and he moves closer.
JANE does not reciprocate; nor does she move away.

I owe you a debt.

JANE   There's no debt, sir.

Beat. He is looking at her intently.

ROCHESTER   I knew you would do me good when I first beheld you.

JANE   I'm glad I happened to be awake.

ROCHESTER is pulling JANE closer and she doesn't resist…

ROCHESTER   My guardian angel…

…until, remembering herself, JANE backs away.

What? You *will* go?

JANE   I'm cold, sir.

ROCHESTER waits for a long moment then reluctantly lets her go.

ROCHESTER   Yes. You are cold. Goodnight then.

He exits. JANE turns to the audience.

JANE   *(To audience)* The rest of the night passed quietly, but I didn't sleep. Till morning dawned I was tossed on a buoyant but unquiet sea, where billows of trouble rolled under surges of joy.

The stage is reconfigured. FAIRFAX enters with blackened bed curtains.

(*To FAIRFAX*) Mrs. Fairfax? Where's
Mr. Rochester?

FAIRFAX turns.

FAIRFAX   Gone.

JANE   Gone?

FAIRFAX   First light. Snored until dawn on the
library sofa, saddled his own horse and —
voof! Expect he knew he was going to get
a piece of my mind. Smoking cigars in bed.
Honestly. Look at these curtains! Fit for
rags alone. Here.

FAIRFAX and JANE begin folding the curtains together.

JANE   Is he travelling again?

FAIRFAX   Only to the Leas; ten miles other side of
Millcote. Mr. Eshton's throwing a party.
It's all they do, that lot. Throw parties,
count money and try to avoid gout.
Anyway, don't expect him back for a
week. Two if there are ladies present.
Three if one of them's Blanche Ingram.

JANE   Who's that?

FAIRFAX   Lord Ingram's youngest. Pretty little
thing. Last Christmas ball Mr. Rochester
held, she was by his side the whole night;
singing, dancing, laughing at rubbish like
they do. She's very much the favourite for

his hand, but... there are others in the
shadows if she falls out of favour.

JANE   Oh.

FAIRFAX   Oh yes; the ladies are very fond of our Mr.
Rochester. Money, you see?

JANE   Is it?

FAIRFAX   Lord knows it's not looks.

*FAIRFAX exits with the curtains. Music. As JANE talks the
stage is reconfigured by the rest of the company.*

JANE   *(To audience)* Blanche Ingram. The name
echoed through the chasm within me, and
nothing could fill it; not Adèle's
improvements nor the gossip of the staff.
For the first time since my childhood I felt
real loneliness. The house became a dreary
shell without its master. And when he did
return... he was not alone.

*ROCHESTER and FOUR – now as BLANCHE Ingram –
enter. They form a tableau upstage; the image is of romantic
harmony. ROCHESTER has a glass of wine in one hand; a bottle
in the other.*

                  The party at Mr. Eshton's, it seemed, was
to continue on to Thornfield. I was asked
to attend the first night with Adèle, and
watched them in the day room until Adèle
went to bed. After that, feeling quite out

of place, I found a windowsill in the library and concealed myself.

JANE sits and watches as the scene progresses. BLANCHE plays two notes on the piano.

BLANCHE   Ah! This is perfect. So much more intimate...

ROCHESTER puts the wine and the glass down and moves to BLANCHE.

ROCHESTER   I'm glad you approve.

BLANCHE   I had been waiting for you to prise me away from the throng...

ROCHESTER   Half the enjoyment, Miss Ingram, is anticipation.

BLANCHE   So *you* say; you weren't stuck with Colonel Dent.

ROCHESTER   You were hardly stuck.

BLANCHE   I was down to my last *bon mot*. So...

A beat. BLANCHE moves closer to ROCHESTER.

                   ...allow me to show you my gratitude...

JANE braces herself... but is saved by BLANCHE's mother Mrs. INGRAM (played by THREE), who bundles in saying:

INGRAM   I wasn't aware you were fond of children Mr. Rochester.

BLANCHE   Mother...!

INGRAM	What? I just ran into the little beast.

ROCHESTER moves easily from BLANCHE to INGRAM.

	Take my advice; send her to school at once.
ROCHESTER	No need. I have a governess.
BLANCHE	Was that the dreary looking thing I saw drifting about earlier?
INGRAM	Waste of time and money.
ROCHESTER	Is that so?
INGRAM	Trust me, Mr. Rochester; you save nothing by bringing a capricious incompetent into the house.
BLANCHE	I had over a dozen in my day, didn't I, mother? Half of them detestable, the other half ridiculous. And all incubi.

All laugh, covering:

JANE	*(To herself – and the audience)* Succubi.
BLANCHE	Where is she now? Lurking in a corner no doubt, instead of attending to that *enfant terrible*.
INGRAM	Quite. *(To ROCHESTER)* I studied her face earlier, Mr. Rochester; within it I saw all the faults of her class.
ROCHESTER	What faults are those, Madam?

INGRAM	Blanche can tell you better than I.
BLANCHE	Actually I'd prefer to change the subject entirely. Would you second me on that point, Mr. Rochester?
ROCHESTER	That and any other, Madam.
BLANCHE	Are you in voice tonight, Signor Eduardo?
ROCHESTER	Donna Bianca, if you command it, I will be.
BLANCHE	Then I shall play for you, and you shall sing *con spirito*.
ROCHESTER	As you command.

BLANCHE sits and plays and introduction.

INGRAM	In here? Shouldn't you prefer to play the grand, darling?
BLANCHE	*(Pointedly)* Perhaps in a moment, mother...

INGRAM gets the message; this is part of a seduction.

INGRAM	Ah. Yes; I think I might... catch up with Colonel Dent.

INGRAM exits. ROCHESTER begins to sing.

ROCHESTER	*(Singing)* Some have won a wild delight, By daring wilder sorrow; Could I gain thy love to-night

I'd hazard death to-morrow.

Could the battle-struggle earn
One kind glance from thine eye,
How this withering heart would burn,
The heady fight to try!

Welcome nights of broken sleep
And days of carnage cold,
Could I deem that thou wouldst weep
To hear my perils told.

During this JANE addresses the audience.

JANE   *(To audience)* That she was pretty was undeniable; she shone, in truth – though she didn't seem to have the wit to charm him. Still, was this the sort of woman that Mr. Rochester admired? I'd waited all day for a glance of recognition from him. I received none. And hearing his fine voice soar above Miss Ingram's perfect playing, my feelings were both cruel and beautiful.

They complete their duet.

BLANCHE   A fine rehearsal.

ROCHESTER smiles.

Perhaps now we might present ourselves to the others.

ROCHESTER   Prepare yourself; I'll join you presently.

BLANCHE smiles and exits. ROCHESTER follows but lingers in the doorway.

> *(Without turning)* Jane?

JANE turns into the scene.

> Are you sick?

JANE   Sir?

ROCHESTER   I asked you to be in attendance.

JANE   And I was. I am.

ROCHESTER   Yet not a word to me.

JANE   You seemed occupied.

ROCHESTER   The last time we saw one another was the night of...

A beat.

> Did you not wonder how I was? Not as an employer; as a friend.

JANE   Of course.

ROCHESTER   Then as a friend you could have – *(asked me)*

FAIRFAX enters.

FAIRFAX   You have a visitor, Mr. Rochester.

ROCHESTER reluctantly turns to FAIRFAX.

> A Mr. Mason.

A beat.

> Late of Spanish Town. *(To JANE)* Jamaica.

ROCHESTER takes an involuntary step backward.

> Don't doubt it either. He's refused to take his coat off and is shivering by the fire. He's made some of the guests nervous. There's talk of rabies.

JANE   Who from?

FAIRFAX   I don't know. Some idiot.

ROCHESTER   Thank you, Mrs. Fairfax; I'll... er... bring me... bring me some wine. If you would.

FAIRFAX looks at JANE.

FAIRFAX   You have some there, sir.

FAIRFAX indicates the wine and bottle. ROCHESTER moves over to them as if it's the first time he's seen them.

ROCHESTER   Of... of course. Then... then do me another favour.

FAIRFAX   What now? Whisky?

ROCHESTER looks at her. He is far from amused.

ROCHESTER   Approach our Mr. Mason by the fire. Doesn't matter who he's speaking to or what mood they seem to be in – ask him to join us. Go; now!

With a curtsey FAIRFAX exits, a worried look on her face. ROCHESTER drains and refills his glass. JANE makes to leave, but he signals her to stay. A beat. He drinks again, then says:

Jane, this is a blow.

JANE Sir?

A beat. ROCHESTER finishes his second glass, puts it and the wine bottle down and moves to JANE.

ROCHESTER Tell me, if everyone here were to suddenly spit at and beat me, what would you do?

JANE *(Thrown)* If...?

ROCHESTER What would you do?

JANE Well. Turn them out, sir; if I could.

ROCHESTER And if they whispered coldly and left me, would you go too?

JANE I would stay with you.

ROCHESTER Even if you were hated for it?

JANE Yes.

A beat. ROCHESTER puts his hands lightly on JANE's upper arms and appears to be about to say something, but instead redirects his attention to FAIRFAX, who has entered with MASON, lingering behind her in the doorway.

FAIRFAX Mr. Mason, sir.

FAIRFAX walks past ROCHESTER. They exchange a particular look not lost on JANE, though she cannot discern the meaning of it. FAIRFAX exits. A beat. MASON steps further into the space.

ROCHESTER   Richard.

MASON   Edward.

ROCHESTER   An unexpected pleasure.

MASON   For both of us, I hope.

A pause. Tension.

ROCHESTER   Shall we talk in my study? Thank you... Miss Eyre.

ROCHESTER exits with MASON. Music. The stage is reconfigured and lights change; it is later that night.

JANE   *(To audience)* Without the host, the party soon broke up for the evening. I returned to my room, left the blinds open and sat on the window seat, bathing in moonlight. I'd never seen Mr. Rochester like that before. He seemed almost *scared* by his new guest's presence... and though I tried not to speculate as to why, it was clear that something was wrong. Something was very, very – *(wrong)*

A man's scream cuts JANE off. ROCHESTER's voice from offstage.

ROCHESTER   *(Off)* Jane? Are you up?

JANE   Yes sir.

ROCHESTER	*(Off)* And dressed? May I come in?
JANE	Yes.
	ROCHESTER enters.
ROCHESTER	Do you turn sick at the sight of blood?
JANE	I'm sorry?
ROCHESTER	There's no time to explain; do you turn – *(sick at the sight of blood)*
JANE	No. No.
ROCHESTER	Good. Fetch a sponge or cloth from your room. Volatile salts too, if you have them and meet me by the door to the blue room. Quickly.
JANE	What's – *(the matter?)*
ROCHESTER	Quickly!

Music. ROCHESTER exits in haste. JANE gathers the appropriate things and turns to the audience.

JANE	*(To audience)* Expecting to be shown into the blue room, I was instead rather astonished to see Mr. Rochester pull back the tapestry on the opposite wall, revealing a door I had no knowledge of until that very moment. He produced a key, unlocked this mysterious entrance and led me up a flight of darkened wood stairs to a small chamber with rooms beyond. There, sitting on a chair by a

93

window lit only by a single candle... was Mr. Mason.

MASON enters from the other side. His left arm is soaked with blood and there is a bloody rag round his neck covering a gash. He collapses into a chair as ROCHESTER and JANE approach.

ROCHESTER   Can you dress that wound?

JANE   *(Somewhat stunned)* Can... I...?

ROCHESTER   *(Louder; insistent)* Dress the wound!

MASON stirs at the sound of ROCHESTER's raised voice.

        (Under his breath) Damn it.

ROCHESTER nods at JANE to tend to MASON's arm. As JANE approaches he lurches, suddenly awake and terrified.

        Calm yourself.

MASON   She's done for me...

ROCHESTER   Nonsense.

MASON   She bit me. Said she'd drain my heart...

ROCHESTER   It was foolish to attempt a meeting alone.

MASON   Slashed me with a knife.

ROCHESTER   You should have waited for me.

MASON   I wish I could forget it.

ROCHESTER takes a small bottle from his coat and, uncorking it, helps MASON to drink from it while saying:

ROCHESTER	You will. Head back to Spanish Town; put all this behind you…
MASON	*(Drowsily)* What have you… *(done to her)* what has she… *(become)*?

His head falls to his chest. JANE steps away from MASON.

ROCHESTER	I need you to stay with him a little longer.
JANE	Sir?
ROCHESTER	Give him water if he rouses but nothing else. Most important of all, do not speak to him. Not a word.
JANE	What – *(happened to him?)*
ROCHESTER	You've done what you can but he needs a doctor. I'll have to dispatch the carriage.
JANE	Don't go.
ROCHESTER	I'll come back. I promise.

ROCHESTER moves to an exit and stands framed there; his back to the audience. JANE is alone with MASON.

JANE	*(To audience)* Using the same key, Mr. Rochester moved through an adjoining door, being sure to lock it firmly behind him. My head swam.

She looks around her. Only the wind can be heard.

What was this place? What hid within its walls?

There is the sound of crashing – as if furniture is being trashed – and ROCHESTER turns. MASON stirs faintly and JANE approaches him, checking his neck, his temperature and so on.

As if summoned by my question, Mr. Rochester's voice presented the only answer...

ROCHESTER   Stay there. No! No; Grace! That's it. Now stay there, in God's name! Grace... *Grace!*

A scream is heard. ROCHESTER exits. A beat.

JANE   *(To audience)* After that... nothing.

JANE turns her head away and appears to be on the verge of returning to her seat when, in a flash, MASON shoots an arm out and grabs her, yelling:

MASON   Help me!

A punch of music accompanies the line. JANE screams. Blackout. MASON exits. JANE on the floor. ROCHESTER crouched over her, a whisky bottle in his hand. Lights.

ROCHESTER   Jane.

She rouses and looks at him.

JANE   Where is he?

ROCHESTER   We... I... was able to move him. Are you all right?

JANE   I think so. I must have...

She sits up.

Who did that to him?

ROCHESTER   It was an accident.

JANE   Like the fire?

ROCHESTER doesn't respond.

Tell me about Grace Poole.

ROCHESTER   Remember your place, Miss Eyre.

JANE   Tell me!

Pause.

ROCHESTER   Grace is a... troubled girl. She has a singular nature.

JANE   *Singular nature*? She's never seen, prowls the upstairs at all hours; tried to burn you alive... now she's nearly *killed* one of your guests!

ROCHESTER   There are things you don't understand.

JANE   Then *help* me understand!

Pause.

ROCHESTER   She's the daughter of a former gardener. Cursed with a crippling shyness. She... did me a great service, some years ago, and... I cannot repay that by putting her out on the street. She's alone in the world. Like Adèle. Like you.

JANE processes this as ROCHESTER takes a slug of whisky.

I would never place you in harm's way. Do you believe that?

A beat. JANE does not answer. ROCHESTER slumps in a chair.

You should return to your room. I'll wait for the doctor.

JANE   But if she's capable of – *(doing something like that)*

ROCHESTER   *(With sudden fury)* No more questions tonight!

Music. JANE watches ROCHESTER take a long drink of whisky from the bottle before exiting. She turns to the audience as THREE, FOUR and FIVE reconfigure the space.

JANE   *(To audience)* The next day brought no sign of Mr. Mason. The doctor must have taken him as commanded. Mr. Rochester was up and ready for the hunt – revitalised, no doubt, by the attentions of Miss Ingram, who clung to him like a dewy-eyed limpet.

ROCHESTER enters with BLANCHE on his arm. They stand in tableau, looking at one another.

Society would hail their union as a fine match, no doubt – for many reasons beyond the obvious I did not concur... though by the end of the day I had other things on my mind.

JOHN enters and brings JANE a letter, which she opens and reads. Lights up on ROCHESTER's study. ROCHESTER and BLANCHE enter, sit and laugh together. Their laughter is broken as JANE moves to join them, the letter in her hand and a serious expression on her face.

BLANCHE   What can the creeping creature want now?

JANE   *(To ROCHESTER)* Sir, I must speak with you.

BLANCHE laughs.

BLANCHE   *(Grandly)* "The demands of governesses."

ROCHESTER smiles.

(To JANE) Then do it. And be quick.

Beat. BLANCHE looks at ROCHESTER who smiles apologetically. She kisses him and exits.

ROCHESTER   She's a rare one, is she not?

JANE   If you say so, sir.

A beat.

ROCHESTER   Well?

JANE   I need a leave of absence for a week or two.

A beat.

ROCHESTER   Why, may I ask?

JANE	My... cousin, John Reed, died last month, and it seems that upon hearing the news my Aunt Reed took ill...
ROCHESTER	Aunts? Cousins? You said you had no family.
JANE	She cast me off.
ROCHESTER	Why?
JANE	Because I was poor and burdensome and she disliked me.
ROCHESTER	Then what reason do you have to go to her?
JANE	They fear she may die.

A beat.

ROCHESTER	And where is this lost Aunt?
JANE	Gateshead Hall.
ROCHESTER	That's a hundred miles away! When will you go?
JANE	There'll be a coachman waiting for me at the George Inn at Millcote first light tomorrow

A beat.

ROCHESTER	You have it all planned out, don't you?

JANE says nothing. ROCHESTER sighs.

	Promise to return within a week.
JANE	I cannot, sir.
ROCHESTER	You'll not stay indefinitely though. Promise that.
JANE	You have my word.

A beat. He looks at her.

ROCHESTER	Something else...?
JANE	When I return, I... I must seek a situation elsewhere.
ROCHESTER	What?
JANE	I shall advertise.
ROCHESTER	The Devil you will! What nonsense is this?
JANE	You are to be married, sir.
ROCHESTER	What of it?
JANE	When your bride takes residence she'll doubtless wish to have you to herself. At that point Adèle will go to school and my... position... becomes redundant.
ROCHESTER	I see.

A beat.

	Do not advertise.
JANE	Sir, I must!

ROCHESTER   No; let me seek a position for you. And write when you are to return. I'll send a coach for you.

ROCHESTER stands.

How will Thornfield survive without you, Jane Eyre?

JANE   I'm sure that it will, sir.

They hold a look for a moment, then ROCHESTER holds his hand out quite formally.

ROCHESTER   I wish you Godspeed.

He exits. JANE rubs at the hand ROCHESTER just shook as the company reconfigure the space around her, recreating the sitting room at Gateshead Hall.

JANE   *(To audience)* Parting from Mr. Rochester left me weary and heart-sick all the way to Gateshead Hall. Bessie, my old nursemaid, greeted me warmly; told me what a fine young woman I'd grown into. "A perfect match for any man." I almost burst into tears, but didn't. Those would have to keep until later...

JANE turns to find GEORGIANA sitting.

GEORGIANA   Hello, cousin.

JANE   Georgiana. Are you well?

GEORGIANA   I'm back here, so... not really, no.

JANE	I'm so sorry.
GEORGIANA	I'm sorry too. I'm used to London society, but... *(sighing)* duty takes precedence over pleasure.

A beat.

JANE	Do you know how John – *(met his end?)*
GEORGIANA	Shot himself.

A beat.

He owed money. Mama had been propping him up for years, but... when she couldn't afford to do it anymore, he. Well. Bullies are cowards. John proved no exception.

A beat.

How long do you intend to stay? Or are you here to gloat?

JANE	I intend to help where I can, for as long as needs be.
GEORGIANA	Really?

JANE nods. GEORGIANA stands, crosses to her and embraces her.

Thank you, cousin. Thank you.

JANE smiles.

I shall return to London next week.

JANE	I'm sorry?
GEORGIANA	I'll doubtless be in the way, so... I think. Yes. I think that's for the best.

She moves to the door.

> I should pack my things. Until later, cousin.

She exits. JANE turns to the audience.

JANE	*(To audience)* Staying with Aunt Reed was a distraction from my troubles, but not a pleasurable one – a familiar cruelty held sway over what was left of her mind...

AUNT REED enters, walking with a cane.

> *(To AUNT REED)* You shouldn't be up, aunt.

AUNT REED	Who is it? Who's there? Bessie?
JANE	Not Bessie. Jane. Eyre.
AUNT REED	Jane Eyre? I've had more trouble with that child than anyone would believe. Such a burden she was. I wish she'd died.

JANE eases her into a chair.

> And now there's John. So much money he owes. I'll write to him; tell him to come home.

JANE	No; aunt…
AUNT REED	I can keep him better here, Bessie.
JANE	Aunt. It's me.

A slight recognition.

AUNT REED	Jane?

JANE nods.

	In the box on the dresser. A letter.
JANE	For me?
AUNT REED	From your Uncle. John Eyre.

A beat.

	Wanted to adopt you. Take you to Madeira, where he was a successful merchant. Give you a more fulfilling life. Bequeath everything to you.

A beat. JANE has retrieved the letter. She is looking at it.

	(Bitterly) To *you.*
JANE	This is… three years old. Why wasn't – *(I told about this)*
AUNT REED	I replied for you.
JANE	You…?
AUNT REED	*(Quoting)* "Dear sir, I am afraid there was an outbreak of typhus at Lowood School, where your niece was a pupil.

She turns and appears to look at JANE.

> Jane Eyre... is dead."

A beat.

JANE   Why?

AUNT REED   You think I was going to... see Jane Eyre placed in a state of ease and comfort? After how she turned on me as a child?

She laughs.

> I've made my peace with my actions and prepare even now for the hereafter; whether it's to heaven or the other place I go...

A pause. JANE crouches before AUNT REED.

> *(Calling off)* Bessie? Who is this? Bessie?

JANE   I'd have been glad to love you if you'd let me.

AUNT REED   Go away.

JANE   You have my forgiveness, aunt. Ask now for God's and be at peace.

JANE goes to kiss AUNT REED, who turns away. JANE moves to the door.

AUNT REED   Jane Eyre.

JANE looks back at her, almost with hope.

I hate her.

AUNT REED exits. Music underscores, possibly incorporating a funeral bell.

JANE   *(To audience)* Aunt Reed clung on bitterly for another ten days. I made all arrangements, attended the funeral and left. I also wrote to my Uncle in Madeira, informing him that I was very much alive.

Music swells. The stage is reconfigured.

Mr. Rochester was as good as his word – the day after the funeral William was driving me back to Thornfield in a beautiful, brand new carriage. This gave me heart, though by the time we passed the Leas and pushed on towards Millcote I could think only of Blanche Ingram slamming the gate in my face, a wedding ring sparkling on her finger. I thought I might alight early; approach the grounds on foot, but instead the coach took a sharp left and pulled hard up a rough path that led to a tangle of trees. At the edge of the copse it stopped. I stepped down.

JANE turns.

William? What is this place?

ROCHESTER enters.

ROCHESTER   Don't you recognise it?

107

JANE cannot speak.

> We'll be fine from here, William.

The sound of a carriage heading off into the distance. ROCHESTER gazes at JANE.

> What did you think of the carriage?

JANE cannot answer.

> It was commissioned in London. A perfect vessel for Mrs. Rochester.

JANE sways a little. ROCHESTER smiles.

> Calm; you have missed no wedding. I couldn't marry without you.

JANE looks around. She says nothing. She is fighting tears.

> At least tell me you're glad to be home.

She can't say it.

> I'm glad you are. Mrs. Fairfax too. And foolish little Adèle is fairly frothing at the mouth.

JANE smiles weakly.

> Now, are you still set on seeking a new situation?

JANE   I fear I must, sir.

ROCHESTER Then I have news.

JANE	When the order to march comes, I'll be ready.
ROCHESTER	I must give that order tonight.
JANE	Oh.

A beat.

ROCHESTER	Have you been happy at Thornfield?
JANE	Of course. I have been well-treated there. Never persecuted; never shunned. It's been my home. I have lived a... a full and delightful life within its... walls.

A beat. JANE steals herself. This has got to be said.

> And I have talked – face to face – with one who has treated me as an equal. It strikes me with... with *terror* to feel I must be torn from you forever.

ROCHESTER	What is this "must?" Why *must* you?
JANE	Because you are to marry Miss Ingram! A noble and beautiful woman will be your bride, and I... I... won't... *(see you again)*

She turns away from him, distraught.

ROCHESTER	My bride will never turn anyone away. It's not her nature.

He comes up close behind her.

> Stay.

JANE   I cannot.

ROCHESTER   If it's your home…

She turns on him, passions roused.

JANE   I tell you I cannot! How could I? Do you
                  think I want to become nothing to you?
                  Do you think I am an automaton? A
                  machine without feelings? Do you think
                  because I am poor, plain and little, I have
                  no soul, no heart? I have as much soul as
                  you and full as much heart and if I had
                  beauty and wealth, I would make it as
                  hard for you to leave me as it is for me to
                  leave you. But you are as good as married
                  to a woman I know you don't love and I
                  scorn you for it.

ROCHESTER kisses her but JANE shoves him forcefully away.

                  No! I am no bird and no net ensnares me;
                  I am a free human being with an
                  independent will, which I now exert to
                  leave you.

ROCHESTER catches her as she tries to leave.

                  Let me go! Marry Miss Ingram and let me
                  go.

ROCHESTER   I have not been speaking of Miss Ingram.

He lets JANE go and stares at her.

                  I spoke of you. I love you.

JANE   I will not be made a fool of.

ROCHESTER   I would never do that. Certainly not here,
                  of all places.

He urges JANE to look around.

                  These last few weeks I have visited this
                  copse more times than I can count. It is the
                  most important place in the world to me.
                  Just there; where you're standing... is
                  where I first saw you. And here – the spot
                  where I fell.

JANE looks at him.

                  I fell.

A beat.

                  My heart is bonded to yours. It's you I
                  wish to marry.

JANE   Stop.

ROCHESTER   The carriage was for you; the new
                  situation by my side.

JANE   Stop this farce!

A beat.

ROCHESTER   Do you doubt me?

JANE   Entirely

ROCHESTER   You have no faith?

JANE	Not a whit.
ROCHESTER	Then let me speak – what happens after shall be your choice.

Pause.

Since our... chance encounter in this wood, I have felt something... as if there's a, a string. Here.

He touches his heart.

And that string – which has never felt any connection before... was at once inextricably knotted to a similar string in you.

A beat.

My heart beats with yours. Every skip; every flutter. Tell me you feel it too.

JANE moves to ROCHESTER and kisses him passionately. Music. As the lights fade, we see BERTHA in a black veil staring from the wood. Blackout.

End of Act One

ACT TWO.

The stage has been reconfigured during the interval; a broken, blackened dressing table is positioned in a downstage corner. The frame is empty. One of the mismatched chairs/stools sits behind it. JANE sits at the mirror, brushing her hair. She looks content. Music plays; a pretty ballad. The company sings:

COMPANY   If thou be in a lonely place,
If one hour's calm be thine,
As evening bends her placid face
O'er this sweet day's decline;
If all the earth and all the heaven
Now look serene to thee,
As o'er them shuts the summer even,
One moment think of me!

Pause, in the lane, returning home;
'Tis dusk, it will be still:
Pause near the elm, a sacred gloom
Its breezeless boughs will fill.
Look at that soft and golden light,
High in the unclouded sky;
Watch the last bird's belated flight,
As it flits silent by.

And well my dying hour were blest,
If life's expiring breath
Should pass, as thy lips gently prest
My forehead, cold in death;
And sound my sleep would be, and sweet,
Beneath the churchyard tree,
If sometimes in thy heart should beat
One pulse, still true to me.

ROCHESTER enters and stares at her from the doorway.

ROCHESTER   I'm aware it's a break in tradition…

JANE   *(To audience)* It is a month later.

ROCHESTER   …but I will not have my entry denied.

JANE   *(To audience)* The night before the wedding.

She turns to him.

(To ROCHESTER) You can't be here.

ROCHESTER   Rather here than out there; it's brewing up for a storm.

JANE   You know what I mean.

ROCHESTER   Did I not say I wanted to stay up with you the night before I put my old bachelor's neck into the sacred noose…?

JANE hits him playfully.

…enter the holy estate of matrimony.

JANE   That was when you were marrying Miss Ingram.

ROCHESTER   Oh, Miss Ingram. Discovering her true nature was easy enough. I put out a rumour that my fortune was not a third of what was supposed and watched her affections dissipate like smoke in the wind.

                          And I never loved her; you were right
                          about that.

JANE   Even so. It's still bad luck.

ROCHESTER   Leave luck to the luckless; I shall prowl
                          where I may...

*He moves to JANE; she allows him to embrace her momentarily.
There is the distant rumble of thunder.*

JANE   Not tonight.

She breaks the embrace.

                          Tell me where you've been.

ROCHESTER   And spoil the surprise?

He kisses her, then turns away.

                          Things to arrange, that's all.

JANE   How many more things are there to
                          arrange? The dresses, the flowers...

ROCHESTER   Nothing for you to worry about.

JANE   *(Teasing)* As you wish, sir.

*He turns back to see JANE affect a small curtsey. He rolls his eyes.
Smiling, JANE sits at her dressing table again and returns to
brushing her hair. Another rumble of thunder; this time a little
louder. ADELE enters, distressed. She dashes past
ROCHESTER and hurls herself at JANE, clinging to her legs,
looking up at her. She is distraught.*

ROCHESTER   What the Devil – ?

JANE Adèle? What's the matter?

ROCHESTER *(Annoyed)* Why aren't you in bed?

JANE looks at him. He turns away.

JANE Is it the storm?

ADELE Dis-moi que ce n'est pas vrai! S'il vous plait, mademoiselle. S'il vous plait!

FAIRFAX enters, quite out of breath.

FAIRFAX Here you are, you little –

She stops when she sees ROCHESTER is present.

Beg your pardon, sir.

ROCHESTER *(Deadpan)* No, no; the more the merrier.

ADELE *(To ROCHESTER; upset & angry)* Taisez-vous! Traitre!

ROCHESTER Traitor?

JANE How is he a traitor?

FAIRFAX Come – come on now, little one...

ADELE Madame Fairfax say... that *he* want to take you away for a year and more, so that I see you no more...

ROCHESTER looks at FAIRFAX.

FAIRFAX It slipped out.

ROCHESTER Slipped out?

116

FAIRFAX   I thought she'd be excited for the pair of
                     you; long honeymoon away…

*A beat. FAIRFAX realises that if the surprise wasn't blown before
it is now.*

JANE   What's this?

JANE looks at ROCHESTER.

ROCHESTER   Surprise.

Everything is quiet for a moment; then:

FAIRFAX   Pop her back in bed then, shall I?

ROCHESTER and JANE are just staring at one another.

                     (Almost to herself) Yes; think that's best.
                     Yes.

*She holds her hand out to summon ADELE. She shakes her head
but JANE whispers something in her ear. ADELE hugs JANE
tight then runs to FAIRFAX and, with a last furious glance at
ROCHESTER, they exit. JANE and ROCHESTER look at one
another, then laugh and come together. They hold one another.
Louder thunder.*

JANE   Where are we going?

ROCHESTER   London first; then Paris, Vienna, Rome…

JANE   Rome?

*There is a slight gasp from offstage. ADELE is eavesdropping.
ROCHESTER raises his voice intentionally.*

ROCHESTER   *(Louder)* And after, we'll go to the Moon;
                       find a white cave and stay there, just you
                       and I. Forever.

ADELE cries from offstage:

ADELE   *(Off)* There is no air on the Moon; you will
                       starve her!

JANE cannot help but smile. ROCHESTER yells:

ROCHESTER   *(Mock aggravation)* Get to your room!

ADELE screams and laughs.

                       Why did you not let me send her away?

JANE   It would have been too much, and too soon
                       – you know that. I enjoy being Adèle's
                       governess. And I have a great love for her.

ROCHESTER   Your capacity for love is endless, it seems.

JANE   Lucky for you that it is.

*He frowns at her. It is not aggressive. A loud clap of thunder.
JANE starts a little.*

ROCHESTER   Don't worry. It'll clear the air for the
                       morning.

*She sits and brushes her hair again. He puts a hand on her
shoulder. Caresses her.*

JANE   It seems unreal.

ROCHESTER   What?

JANE   You. This. All that's happening.

ROCHESTER   I'm real enough.

JANE   You're the most phantom-like of all.

A beat.

ROCHESTER   You strange, unearthly creature.
                  Tomorrow I'm yours utterly.

*She stands and turns to him. He regards her and they smile at one
another. She offers her hand which he takes and kisses tenderly.*

                  Goodnight, Miss Eyre. For the last time.

*He exits. JANE turns back to the mirror. Music. She sings to
herself as she tries on her veil. It ought to be a sweet image;
something beautiful but innocuous... that is at once shattered – the
music immediately becoming darker. Ominous bass tones;
discordant strings. Lights change too – and there, upstage in a tight
spotlight cutting through the darkness, is BERTHA, all in black,
wearing the tattered black veil she wore in Act One. This image is
held for a couple of beats only.*

JANE   *(Calling)* Edward? There's someone...
                  someone's in my room!

*The same image except this time BERTHA is closer. JANE looks
terrified.*

JANE   Help! Help me!

BERTHA is closer now, she stares at JANE.

JANE   Who are you? What do you want from me?

The music is down to a pulse. JANE looks in the direction she had been looking. Thunder rumbles.

JANE   Adèle…?

In the blackout BERTHA removes and secretes the veil. She is FAIRFAX once again.

FAIRFAX   Jane. Jane…

Lights slowly creep up. FAIRFAX is gently shaking JANE's shoulder.

ROCHESTER   *(Off)* Jane?

Lights up full now. It is early morning. JANE looks at FAIRFAX.

FAIRFAX   Dear me, you look dreadful. Have you slept there all night?

JANE looks around her.

JANE   I…

FAIRFAX   Best get a move on. The master's been calling you.

JANE stands and moves to the puppet.

JANE   She was here. It was real!

ROCHESTER   *(Off)* Jane!

FAIRFAX   Have you been dreaming?

JANE   No. I don't think so. I think Grace Poole was in here. Last night. With this.

FAIRFAX   No. That's not possible.

JANE   Why not?

ROCHESTER enters before any answer can be given. He looks anxious.

ROCHESTER   What's going on up here?

FAIRFAX   Give the lass a minute or two to come round, sir. Please.

ROCHESTER   Why?

FAIRFAX   I fear she's had a nightmare.

ROCHESTER   She looks as fair as a lily. Is William preparing the carriage?

FAIRFAX   He was harnessing the horses when I left him.

ROCHESTER   Luggage?

FAIRFAX   They'll be loaded on once William's done.

ROCHESTER   It must be ready the moment we return: boxes and luggage arranged and strapped on...

FAIRFAX joins in with the last part of the sentence.

                    (with FAIRFAX) ...and the coachman in his seat.

FAIRFAX   Yes. I know.

ROCHESTER takes JANE's hand.

ROCHESTER   Jane? The clergyman will be waiting.

JANE   Yes... I... of course...

She smiles at him weakly. His stern and nervous face scares her.

ROCHESTER   Good. Come on!

Music. They take a step forward. FAIRFAX exits. Lights. During this next, FOUR and FIVE reconfigure the stage, getting rid of the dressing table and clearing the space to resemble a small village church. JANE addresses the audience.

JANE   *(To audience)* My wrist in a grip of iron we marched to the church at the bottom of the estate. *(To ROCHESTER)* Slow down.

ROCHESTER   No time.

JANE   What's the matter?

ROCHESTER   Nothing.

They take another lurching step.

JANE   *(To audience)* I was pulled so hard I almost fell. His face was more fixed, more stern than I'd ever seen it. We reached the church. A handful of yawning villagers sat witness as the priest stood ready to receive us.

ROCHESTER draws JANE downstage centre and holds her hand. He looks out as if at a priest.

ROCHESTER   What are you waiting for? Begin.

JANE	*(To audience)* I ought to have been ecstatic. Instead my eyes searched the face I had grown to love with terrified concern.
MASON	*(Off)* Rochester!
ROCHESTER	I said begin.
JANE	*(To audience)* I had seen his expression before.
MASON	*(Off)* Edward Rochester!
JANE	*(To audience)* The night of the blood.
ROCHESTER	The vows. Now.
MASON	*(Off)* Stop this! Stop everything!
JANE	*(To audience)* The screaming.
ROCHESTER	Now!
JANE	*(To audience)* The night of Mason.

MASON enters upstage.

MASON	I see an impediment.
ROCHESTER	Ignore him.
MASON	This man has a wife.

ROCHESTER closes his eyes. JANE looks at him questioningly.

> Edward Fairfax Rochester is already married. To my sister.

123

At this and with a roar, ROCHESTER launches himself at MASON, one hand grabbing him by the lapel, the other fixing around his throat.

ROCHESTER   I could squeeze the life out of you. Crush your throat like a bird's egg.

JANE   Edward!

MASON   Someone!

ROCHESTER   How could you?

MASON   Help!

JANE   Edward, stop!

ROCHESTER   How *could* you?

JANE   *(Roaring)* Enough!

This seems to bring ROCHESTER back to his senses.

Enough.

ROCHESTER lets MASON go. MASON falls to his knees. JANE stares at ROCHESTER. Silence. Eventually:

ROCHESTER   Come, then. Come and meet my wife.

Music. The cast – all but THREE – create the third floor together, turning chairs over, taking things out of the rubble and so on. JANE and ROCHESTER remain in an upstage corner of the space; FOUR and FIVE exit. BERTHA enters wearing a tattered shawl over her dress and the black veil, and carrying a dirty, tattered soldier puppet. She sits and moves it, transfixed. JANE and ROCHESTER enter the space.

> Behold. My bride.

BERTHA drops the puppet, pulls the veil from her face and looks at JANE.

JANE   *(Quietly)* No. No. No...

Hearing JANE's voice, BERTHA approaches slowly and with threat. ROCHESTER puts himself between BERTHA and JANE. BERTHA approaches ROCHESTER. Puts her hands on him – it is dangerous but sensual; ROCHESTER stays very still.

ROCHESTER   Don't move.

At once, with a howling laugh, BERTHA claws at ROCHESTER. He is expecting it and catches her hands, but she is strong and pushes him onto his back foot.

> Stay behind me.

BERTHA snarls and tries to bite ROCHESTER's neck – again, it could be construed as sensual but is the act of a deranged mind.

> *(Calling)* Grace?

At the mere mention of her name BERTHA changes, looking back at ROCHESTER accusingly; with upset. FOUR enters. She is GRACE Poole. Her face and arms are covered in scratches. She guides BERTHA away from JANE and settles her in a downstage corner, rocking her. JANE looks at ROCHESTER. He is lost for words. JANE moves to GRACE.

JANE   Did she do that to you?

GRACE does not reply; stroking BERTHA's hair instead.

Grace?

GRACE looks to ROCHESTER who nods, giving her leave to speak.

GRACE Y-yes.

JANE And your eye...?

GRACE nods. Silence.

ROCHESTER She seems... calmer now.

GRACE A. Little.

Pause.

ROCHESTER Thank you. Thank you, Grace. You can... return to your chambers.

With a nod to both ROCHESTER and JANE, GRACE exits. Pause.

Jane, if I could – *(have my time again I'd tell you it all)*

JANE Why?

A beat.

ROCHESTER Why what?

JANE Any of it!

Silence.

ROCHESTER My father... was an ambitious man. He loved two things above all else; my elder brother... and money. I was...

126

He shakes his head; lost for words temporarily. A beat.

> In Jamaica, where he conducted his business, was a family – the Masons. Wealthier than ours. Well connected. Overtones had been made about a union between our two houses, and...

ROCHESTER looks at BERTHA.

> ...they had a daughter.

He pauses as BERTHA giggles, though the sound is far from joyous.

> She was beautiful once; the envy of all Spanish town. And I was... dazzled. More than dazzled; she... ignited... something within me; I cannot deny that.

ROCHESTER looks to JANE who remains impassive. He continues.

> We were married before my father's signature was dry on the contract. Before he and my brother left me alone. Before I discovered the truth.

As if to punctuate the story BERTHA gives a solitary laugh.

> Madness runs in the Mason bloodline. Her mother had it. Her youngest brother. And, gradually... she succumbed too.

A beat.

And they knew. My father and brother. They knew. All along. They knew her mother had not fled the family; that she was in an asylum. They knew her brother's tempers led to his death. They knew the Masons wanted her off their hands. So.

BERTHA cranes her head to look at him.

They sold my liberty for £30,000.

JANE And you let them.

ROCHESTER I was young.

JANE As young as me?

ROCHESTER I didn't have the wisdom you're blessed with at that age.

JANE scoffs.

I was alone, unsupported, and... afraid. There. I was afraid. But I tried; God knows I... four years we stayed together – four years in that place, watching her lustful tempers transform her into...

BERTHA starts to wail; it is a lonely, angry sound. ROCHESTER turns away. GRACE enters soundlessly. She approaches BERTHA and wrestles her to her feet. BERTHA resists; scratching, trying to bite. GRACE exits with her. The wailing stops. Pause.

JANE Tell me about Grace. Why have you made her into this, this...

ROCHESTER	She offered.

A beat.

Grace has always felt uneasy in wide, open spaces. She would cry; howl... after her father died, she got worse. Didn't want to leave; said she could help. I probably – I should have refused but...

A beat.

They're two misfits together. I'm sorry; I shouldn't – *(have said that)*

JANE	Who knows about this?
ROCHESTER	Mrs. Fairfax alone. The staff that saw Bertha arrive has long since been replaced. I swore her to secrecy. Please don't consider her actions a betrayal.
JANE	No-one else has even guessed?
ROCHESTER	Did you?

Pause.

I've no respect for myself in this, Jane. I know what I am. I was close to... to the end when I made my decision.

JANE	To lock her up?
ROCHESTER	To return to Thornfield. I could tell you that I thought the climate might help...

but that would be a lie, and I don't want
to...

He tails off. JANE simply stares at him. A beat.

I hid her. That's what I did. Hid her. Like
a coward. And ran like a child. To Europe;
to the Americas... anywhere. I drank.
Caroused. Gambled. Took women to my
bed. Adèle's mother being one. Nothing
would assuage me. Until you.

A beat.

JANE   I don't know you.

ROCHESTER   Jane...

JANE   Not really.

ROCHESTER   Please...

JANE   I made you my world. My whole world.

ROCHESTER   The feelings I expressed to you... when
                      I... from the moment I saw you on Hay
                      Lane; as I fell from my horse...

JANE   I don't think you should talk of that any
                      more, sir.

ROCHESTER   I meant every word.

JANE   You're a married man.

ROCHESTER   In whose eyes?

JANE   In God's eyes! In mine!

130

ROCHESTER   Insanity is no grounds for divorce!

A beat.

> I did what I thought was best. I couldn't... love her, but... to send her away... if I could free myself I would. Then we...

ROCHESTER reaches out to JANE. She turns away.

> Why don't we leave Thornfield? Take some time to... I have another property near here; Ferndean. We could – *(live there)*

JANE   No.

ROCHESTER   Or... Italy. I could take you to... I have – *(a townhouse in Genoa)*

JANE   I will play mistress for no-one.

A beat.

ROCHESTER   You don't love me then?

JANE   I do. Perhaps more than ever, but...

A beat. This is hard to say.

> ...I cannot be near you.

ROCHESTER   You're going to leave?

A beat.

JANE   Yes.

ROCHESTER is overwhelmed with despair.

ROCHESTER   Please. Please. I know you feel as I do.

He shakes her, presses his lips against hers. She does not respond. When he stops, she turns her head away.

> Do you intend to go one way in the world and let me go another?

JANE looks at him. A beat.

JANE   I do.

ROCHESTER   I will be bitter and broken without my love. You will take all happiness with you.

ROCHESTER is broken. On hearing this, JANE's resolve almost breaks too but she gathers herself together and manages:

JANE   I… will take nothing but myself, sir.

JANE turns from ROCHESTER to hide her own anguishes. He reaches out to touch her shoulder but cannot quite bring himself to do so. He exits. JANE wipes her eyes and addresses the audience.

JANE   *(To audience)* I slept fitfully and left before dawn by the servant's entrance.

She collects a shawl and a purse from the rubble and heads downstage as FAIRFAX enters with a pail.

FAIRFAX   Jane?

JANE stops and turns. A beat.

> We should have told you the truth; I know that.

JANE smiles sadly at FAIRFAX – there is no blame. FAIRFAX puts down the pail and crosses to JANE.

> Come here, lass.

She embraces JANE warmly.

> Whatever you might think of him, he does love you.

They separate. JANE looks at her.

JANE　　　　　Look after Adèle.

FAIRFAX　　　I'll do my best.

JANE turns downstage.

> Where will you go?

JANE　　　　　To the Devil.

Music. A sequence. FAIRFAX exits. During this sequence we hear ROCHESTER who, at a suitably poignant moment in the music, calls:

ROCHESTER　　Jane? Jane! Jane!

The stage is reconfigured. JANE sobs. The music fades to underscore as THREE, FOUR and FIVE speak lines in the abstract; representing the time JANE spends living rough.

FIVE　　　　　*(As COACHDRIVER)* Twenty shillings-'ll get you as far as Whitcross, Miss.

FOUR	*(As SHOPKEEPER)* Been caught in the rain, have you?
FIVE	*(As COACHDRIVER)* You've still a walk from there to reach a town.
JANE	Thank you…
THREE	*(As CHILD)* Mam…?
FOUR	*(As SHOPKEEPER)* If you can't pay for that you'd best put it back.
JANE	Sorry…
THREE	*(As CHILD)* Mam?
FIVE	*(As MAN)* We don't require servants here, thank you.
JANE	Sorry… sorry…
FOUR	*(As SHOPKEEPER)* You again. I've said before…
THREE	*(As CHILD)* Mam! There's a beggar woman here!
FIVE	*(As MAN)* You'll not find anyone round here that does.
FOUR	*(As SHOPKEEPER)* I can't trade bread.
THREE	*(As CHILD)* She's eating t' porridge from 't pig's trough!
JANE	Please… take these gloves…

FOUR	*(As SHOPKEEPER)* No!
JANE	I need shelter…
FIVE	*(As MAN)* No!
JANE	I'm starving…
THREE	*(As CHILD)* No!

JANE groans. Now THREE, FOUR and FIVE are gathered together and looking at her. ROCHESTER gives a final, almighty:

ROCHESTER	Jane!
COMPANY	The human heart has hidden treasures
	In secret kept; in silence sealed –
	The thoughts, the hopes, the dreams, the pleasures,
	Whose charms were broken if revealed.
	Then in our souls there seems to languish
	A tender grief that is not woe;
	And thoughts that once wrung groans of anguish
	Now cause but some mild tears to flow.

He exits, and those present onstage become MARY (THREE), DIANA (FOUR) and ST. JOHN Rivers. The music changes. Lights alter. ST. JOHN is sitting in a chair sipping tea. MARY is at his side. DIANA is closest to JANE, crouching close to her as she sleeps.

ST. JOHN	Who is she?
DIANA	We think her name is Jane.

ST. JOHN	You think?
DIANA	We've not extracted much from her.
MARY	Only that she's travelled a long way.
DIANA	Yes, and that she's been sleeping savage for over a week. She'd had to beg for food.
ST. JOHN	That would explain the state of her.
MARY	She looked far worse when we found her.
DIANA	We had to bathe her. Wash her clothes.
ST. JOHN	What have I told you about letting in strangers while I'm away?
DIANA	It's charity, St. John.
MARY	*(Quoting)* "Blessed is the one who is kind to the needy."
DIANA	The needy; exactly.

A beat.

ST. JOHN	*(To JANE)* Jane, is it?

JANE doesn't move. ST. JOHN stands and moves over to her.

	This is Moor House.
DIANA	She knows.
ST. JOHN	My name is St. John Rivers.
DIANA	She knows that too.

MARY   We've told her all about you.

ST. JOHN   I am a clergyman.

DIANA and MARY look at one another. They've clearly mentioned this as well.

                    These are my sisters –

MARY   St. John we've told – *(her our names)*

DIANA   Just let him do it.

ST. JOHN   Mary and Diana Rivers. You are welcome here. "Do not neglect to do good and to share what you have," saith the Lord in Hebrews. This, at least until you are well enough to tell us whence you came, we shall do.

DIANA   St. John!

ST. JOHN   What more can we do? We know barely anything about her. We don't even know her surname.

JANE   Elliott.

ST. JOHN   I beg your pardon?

JANE   My name is Elliott. Jane Elliott.

Music. Lights drop a little onstage. JANE stands and moves to the chair ST. JOHN was sitting in. MARY gives her a bowl and spoon. She crouches at her feet with some crocheting. DIANA stands by the other side of her, reading from a bible. Upstage, ST. JOHN paces.

DIANA	"I was hungry and you gave me food. I was thirsty and you gave me water. I was a stranger and you welcomed me."
JANE	Matthew. Chapter 25.

A beat.

DIANA	Right again! That's thirteen in a row.
ST. JOHN	The bible should be for contemplation, education and exaltation, not parlour tricks.

DIANA silently mocks ST. JOHN's serious tone to MARY, who has to stifle a giggle.

	(To JANE) It's clear you are an educated woman Miss Elliott.
JANE	Some might say so.
DIANA	Oh! St. John; do you think she might be...

DIANA dashes up to ST. JOHN and whispers in his ear.

ST. JOHN	Far too early to tell. I've known her less than a week.

DIANA looks disappointed.

	"If we hope for what we do not see, we wait for it with patience."
JANE	Romans. Chapter Eight.
MARY	Fourteen.

ST. JOHN   *(Chiding)* Mary!

MARY   You said it.

She smiles at him sweetly. Lights. Music. Same as before. JANE and MARY now sit opposite one another on the floor playing cards. DIANA takes JANE's bowl and exits. ST. JOHN is pulling on a coat.

ST. JOHN   *(Calling off)* Diana? Have you seen my sermon notes?

DIANA   *(Off)* Er...

QUIETLY, and to JANE.

MARY   *(Imitating ST. JOHN)* Not to worry; I shall recite them from memory.

ST. JOHN   *(Calling off)* Not to worry; I shall recite them from memory.

MARY and JANE share a secret smile ST. JOHN moves towards an exit.

Mary. Miss Elliott.

MARY does not respond, but JANE stands and moves to ST. JOHN.

JANE   Mr. Rivers?

ST. JOHN turns.

I only wanted to say that this last month has... renewed my faith in humanity. I am in your debt; yours and your sisters both.

139

ST. JOHN	There is no debt.
MARY	Not to him, but you can come and finish this hand if you like.

JANE smiles. ST. JOHN makes to exit. Music and lights as before. Now ST. JOHN sits in one chair, JANE another, DIANA knits in a chair upstage and MARY reads on the floor downstage. JANE is drawing in a small notebook.

ST. JOHN	What are you sketching?
JANE	Something from memory.
ST. JOHN	Might I see?
JANE	Of course.

He stands.

ST. JOHN	Is that a real house?
JANE	Thornfield Hall.
ST. JOHN	You draw as if you know it well.

JANE does not reply.

MARY	She's really good, isn't she?
ST. JOHN	Well; er... well...

MARY makes a series of harrumphing noises, mimicking ST. JOHN's uncertainty.

> Are you all right, sister? You sound like you have a cough.

MARY smiles and shakes her head. He returns to his seat.

Have you any experience of teaching, Miss
Elliott?

DIANA puts her knitting down. She wants to hear this.

JANE   Some. Two years at Lowood School,
                      before…

A beat.

ST. JOHN   Before…?

*JANE does not reply. DIANA joins ST. JOHN, sensing the
awkwardness.*

DIANA   Lowood School. That's Reverend
                      Brocklehurst's place, isn't it?

JANE   He remains as treasurer only.

ST. JOHN   I've met him once or twice. A dry man;
                      constantly talking about mortification of
                      the flesh. Quite humourless.

MARY almost bursts out laughing but saves herself.

                      And will you be seeking work? Now you
                      are well enough?

JANE   I will.

ST. JOHN   Teaching?

JANE   Anything honest.

DIANA nudges her brother.

DIANA   Tell her, St. John. Please!

ST. JOHN	I am in charge of the village school in Morton, where my parish is to be found. I require a schoolmistress for a class of girls. She would have a private house in the village where she might live quietly, if humbly. The wage is not large. Nor is the house.
MARY	Well sold, St. John. Sounds marvellous.
JANE	Are you offering me the position?
ST. JOHN	You're more than qualified. And you've been with us for seven weeks now; I can't imagine you have any surprises for us.
DIANA	Oh, say you'll do it. Say you'll stay!
ST. JOHN	Diana! Let Miss Elliott consider her decision.
DIANA	Of course. I'll... just...

DIANA hurries away upstage. Behind her brother's back she silently pleads with JANE to accept and stay.

JANE	You can have my decision now if you like.
ST. JOHN	Oh.
JANE	For the charity you have shown me and a chance at an independent life... I accept!

DIANA squeals with delight and dashes round ST. JOHN's chair to embrace JANE warmly. JANE laughs and returns the embrace. ST. JOHN stands, as does MARY, who pushes in front of ST. JOHN and embraces JANE.

MARY   You'll still visit us, won't you?

JANE   If you like.

MARY and DIANA move aside as ST. JOHN rather formally shakes JANE's hand.

           Thank you. And please; from now on call me Jane.

ST. JOHN   I will.

DIANA   *(Prompting ST. JOHN)* And...

ST. JOHN   ...you may call me St. John.

Music. JANE addresses the audience as the stage is reconfigured.

JANE   *(To audience)* And so it was that I returned to myself... after a fashion; teaching half a dozen local girls in a charity school, close to the church where St. John gave his sermons. The cottage was indeed small – sparsely furnished too; but certainly comfortable enough. Where once I thought I might never feel it again, a slight contentment grew within me.

ST. JOHN and DIANA come forwards, in separate scenes.

ST. JOHN   I'm hearing good reports from the parishioners.

DIANA   Will you be coming to dinner on Sunday?

DIANA exits one way, ST. JOHN another as MARY enters.

JANE   *(To audience)* I visited Moor House often.

MARY   Jane! Jane! I learned a new card game. Want to play?

JANE smiles as MARY exits and ST. JOHN returns.

JANE   *(To audience)* Months passed. My affection for Mary and Diana grew into a sisterly love.

ST. JOHN   Will you take a walk with me... Jane? Across to Marsh Glen?

JANE   *(To audience)* I liked St. John as well, of course. He was young, and handsome – kind, too.

ST. JOHN exits as DIANA enters.

DIANA   First term over. Are you enjoying it?

JANE   *(To audience)* Every evening I returned to my lonely little cottage, even though Mary and Diana begged me to stay.

MARY enters.

MARY   Just one more hand of whist, dear Jane.

DIANA   Please...!

MARY and DIANA exit.

JANE   *(To audience)* I sought their company regularly. They were a shelter to the storm in my head. Once I was back in my lonely little cottage my heart became a bird with a broken wing, desperate to return to the nest, yet knowing it was impossible. My soul boiled with thoughts of Edward Rochester. I hated him; I loved him. I yearned for news of him – I never wanted to hear his name again. Over and over; round and round. I might be rinsing a cup, or in the middle of an English grammar lesson and at once I would be dizzy with the rich smells of tobacco and cologne; my heart would skip and pound – I would even blush on occasion. I heard his laughter or the sound of his footsteps enough times to fancy I should go mad.

She stands as ST. JOHN, MARY and DIANA enter, all carrying presents wrapped in festive paper (or, if it's simpler, brown paper with festive ribbon).

MARY   Merry Christmas Jane.

DIANA   Merry Christmas.

JANE   To you as well. *(To ST. JOHN)* Merry Christmas, St. John.

ST. JOHN   Jane.

MARY thrusts her gift out.

MARY   Open this one first.

JANE does as she is told. It is a compass.

So you'll never get lost on the Moors again.

JANE   That's thoughtful; thank you.

DIANA holds hers out. JANE unwraps it.

                        Oh!

It is Bewick's History of British Birds. JANE is astonished.

                        Bewick's History of British Birds!

DIANA   Yes, well you told us that story of your
                        awful cousin, and I thought you might...
                        is it in poor taste?

JANE   It's wonderful!

ST. JOHN   Now mine, if you please.

JANE opens ST. JOHN's gift. It is a book on how to speak Hindustani.

                        As you know, I'm restless to continue
                        God's work.

DIANA   St. John, you've told her.

ST. JOHN   And hope to depart for Hindustan within
                        the year.

MARY   This is getting ridiculous.

ST. JOHN   The study of another language is always
                        stimulating.

JANE   Thank you.

She sets the gifts aside.

                        I've not finished your present yet.

DIANA	What is it?
JANE	It *will be*... a painting. Of all of you. To hang over the fire here.

A beat.

DIANA	Oh.

She looks upset. MARY too.

JANE	I've heard you say you wanted something there.
MARY	We do...

A beat.

ST. JOHN	This... will be our last Christmas at Moor House.
JANE	Your...?
ST. JOHN	The upkeep is... more than we can afford.
JANE	I didn't know.
MARY	Something he hasn't told you! God be praised!
ST. JOHN	Mary!
DIANA	We had an Uncle – our mother's brother. He died recently. He was our last hope.
JANE	How so?
MARY	His fortune is £20,000. More than enough to... you know.

ST. JOHN	Miss Elliott doesn't need to hear – *(these details)*
MARY	We thought he might have – he and father were in business together you see, and by all accounts he had no family of his own, so...
DIANA	Except... well; turns out they quarrelled. A lot. And there's a mysterious cousin. They ended up with the fortune...
MARY	...we were left ten guineas each.
ST. JOHN	Not inconsiderable.
DIANA	But not enough.

A beat.

MARY	Paint Moor House for us.
JANE	Really?
MARY	Please.
DIANA	Wherever we go we can take home with us.
JANE	I will.
ST. JOHN	Come ladies; the evening service awaits...

ST. JOHN, MARY and DIANA exit. Music.

JANE	*(To audience)* Within a week St. John had moved into the Parsonage, Mary and Diana had taken modest rooms in a nearby town and Moor House stood abandoned.

148

JANE takes a small pocket book and pencil and begins sketching as she addresses the audience.

I remained in Morton; teaching, sketching and fighting the heart within me. I still saw the Rivers, though sadness cast a shadow over their visits. I ached for them; for myself... for Edward... yet I could always lose myself in art. The light from the rear window in the cottage was a poor substitute for the vast frames of Thornfield but it was sufficient.

ST. JOHN enters.

ST. JOHN   Forgive the intrusion.

JANE   *(To audience)* It's now February. *(To ST. JOHN)* I'm actually working on a sketch of you.

She shows him.

ST. JOHN   A poor likeness. Far too handsome.

JANE   Not at all.

He studies the picture for a moment.

ST. JOHN   May I have it?

JANE   Of course.

JANE tears out the picture and hands it to ST. JOHN, who takes it carefully, all the while gazing at her.

Is something the matter?

ST. JOHN sits.

ST. JOHN   Sit with me. I have a tale to tell.

JANE   Gossip from the village? I'm surprised. I rely on your sisters for that normally.

ST. JOHN   It's not that kind of tale.

JANE moves into a chair closer to ST. JOHN.

JANE   I'm intrigued...

ST. JOHN smiles.

ST. JOHN   Twenty years ago or thereabouts, a poor curate fell in love with a rich man's daughter.

JANE   Is this a story or a riddle?

A beat.

ST. JOHN   Both, in part. They married against the advice of all her friends, who consequently disowned her. Before two years passed the pair were dead, leaving a child behind them.

JANE   How awful.

ST. JOHN   Charity carried the child, a girl, to the house of rich relations. She was reared by an aunt-in-law who kept her ten years, wherein she was transferred to a place you know well. Lowood School.

JANE begins to recognise her own story in ST. JOHN's words.

JANE   Go on.

ST. JOHN   From a pupil, she became a teacher, like yourself... after which she left to take up the role of governess... for the ward of a certain Mr. Rochester.

JANE   St. John!

ST. JOHN   Hear me to the end.

JANE nods. She is uncomfortable. ST. JOHN continues.

Of that gentleman's character I know but one thing – he professed to offer honourable marriage to this young girl, and at the altar she discovered he had a wife yet alive, though a lunatic.

JANE is almost shaking.

The governess left Thornfield Hall that very night; every effort to find her since has been in vain... and finding her has become a matter of serious urgency; advertisements have been put in all the papers; I myself received a letter from a solicitor named Briggs who communicated the details I've just imparted.

A beat.

JANE   *(Quietly)* How is he?

ST. JOHN   What was that?

JANE	Mr. Rochester. Is he well?
ST. JOHN	I've no idea; aside from his impropriety he's never mentioned.
JANE	Did no-one go to Thornfield? Did no-one see him?
ST. JOHN	Better that you ask the name of the governess.
JANE	I don't care about the governess!
ST. JOHN	You should.

JANE lowers her head. ST. JOHN removes a piece of paper from his pocket.

I have it here.

He hands the sketch back to JANE. JANE looks in horror at her own name.

Briggs wrote to me of a Jane Eyre. The advertisements demanded a Jane Eyre. I knew a Jane Elliott...

A beat.

I confess I had my suspicions, but it was only now, as you showed me your sketch, that I was certain. You've signed your real name.

He lifts her face to meet his gaze.

Jane Eyre?

152

JANE nods.

> Briggs will be pleased. His search is over at last.

JANE What did he want?

ST. JOHN Merely to tell you that your uncle, Mr. Eyre of Madeira, is dead; that he has left you all his property, and that you are now rich to the tune of twenty thousand pounds.

JANE I... I don't... *(understand)*

ST. JOHN You must prove your identity of course; Briggs has the will and the necessary documents.

JANE And why would... why would he write to you; this solicitor?

A beat.

ST. JOHN Now there he goes into a great deal of detail; simply put, it would appear that your uncle... and *our* uncle... are the same person.

JANE The...?

ST. JOHN You are the "mysterious cousin." Our father was your mother's brother.

A beat.

JANE We...?

ST. JOHN	Yes.
JANE	Yes? Yes?

Laughing, JANE takes ST. JOHN's hands and dances round the room; ST. JOHN participating awkwardly.

	A poor orphan child no longer! St. John – cousin – do you know what this means? Moor House! Moor House is saved!
ST. JOHN	No. No, I couldn't accept that.
JANE	That's why I'm not offering it to you.
ST. JOHN	Quite right. Quite right.
JANE	I'm offering it to your sisters. My cousins! My family!

She dances again.

	Write to them tomorrow; tell them to return at once!
ST. JOHN	I… I don't know…
JANE	I do!

Music. DIANA and MARY enter and embrace JANE warmly. The stage is reconfigured as the company sing.

COMPANY	Lough, vessel, plough the British Main,
	Seek the free ocean's wider plain;
	Leave English scenes and English skies
	Unbind, dissever English ties.

My England's shores are yet in view,
England's skies of tender blue
Are arched above her guardian sea.
I cannot yet remembrance flee.

We are now in an outdoor location. JANE addresses the audience.

JANE   *(To audience)* The next few months were
                 as happy as any I could remember since
                 leaving Thornfield. In Diana and Mary I
                 had at last found family members I truly
                 loved. We spoke and behaved as sisters; all
                 of us.

*A beat. ST. JOHN enters with a shawl. He gives it to JANE as
she continues.*

                 Diana suggested I move in with her and
                 Mary once their brother had departed for
                 Hindustan. By midsummer's eve I
                 discovered that was not what St. John had
                 in mind for me...

ST. JOHN   Thank you for accompanying me.

JANE   I enjoy our walks. And I've grown to love
                 Marsh Glen.

ST. JOHN   Let us rest here.

*JANE sits. ST. JOHN moves downstage and looks out, as if
taking in the view.*

                 (To himself) And I shall see it again in
                 dreams...

JANE	What's that?
ST. JOHN	I go in six weeks. Calcutta. I have taken my berth in an East Indiaman.
JANE	I... I barely know what to say.
ST. JOHN	I am the servant of an infallible Master. It is my glory and joy to take His word to the faithless.
JANE	Your heart is well suited to the task.
ST. JOHN	And what of yours?

A beat.

JANE	*(Uncertain)* Mine?
ST. JOHN	There is a strength in you, Jane. In all you've endured.

A beat.

Come with me to India. God intended you for a missionary's wife.

A beat.

JANE	No. St. John; I...
ST. JOHN	I will care for you, stand by you, teach and instruct you – in my own humble way – and claim you not for my pleasure, but for my Sovereign's service.
JANE	I'm not fit for it.

ST. JOHN	There are none more fit. You're formed for labour, not for love. Your own experiences make that plain.
JANE	My own...?
ST. JOHN	I have studied you this past year, Jane. Watched as you taught, seen your compassion; your patience... and I have listened to your stories of Thornfield; of how the bright-burning flame of your love was, through shame and cruelty, almost turned upon you. The self-sacrifice that you sought at the hands of that man was passionate but misguided. In India, that love can be put to good use; be selfless, endless and rewarded by the Master.

A beat.

JANE	I need... to think; to...
ST. JOHN	Yes. Yes; there is much to think about!

JANE stands.

JANE	So much of what has happened this last year has been down to your charity. I see that. And maybe... maybe it is wrong to hang on to...

A beat.

	I'm prepared to go with you.
ST. JOHN	My prayers have been answered!

157

ST. JOHN puts his arms around JANE. It is forced and awkward.

JANE   As your sister.

ST. JOHN is stopped in his tracks.

ST. JOHN   My...

JANE   Yes.

ST. JOHN   No. No. That does not work at all. Holy matrimony is the only way. It's known that you're not my sister.

JANE   To the people in India?

ST. JOHN   *(Ignoring JANE)* How can a man not yet thirty travel with a girl of nineteen if they are unwed? How can we lead by example if this is the example we set?

JANE   Perhaps the example would be our faith alone.

ST. JOHN   Do you think God will be satisfied with half an oblation? I accept your heart on His behalf; a divided allegiance cannot work.

JANE   You're asking me to give my heart to God?

ST. JOHN   Yes.

JANE   Because you don't want it.

A beat.

You don't love me, St. John. Not in the way a husband should love a wife. It may suit you to see me as a fellow-soldier in this endeavour; a comrade, a neophyte...

ST. JOHN   I've never denied you have a woman's heart!

JANE   Not where you're concerned.

A beat.

ST. JOHN   You would not repent marrying me. And enough of love will follow our union to – *(satisfy you)*

JANE   I scorn your idea of love. I scorn the counterfeit sentiment you offer, and I scorn you when you offer it.

ST. JOHN   You scorn only God.

JANE   Love is more natural; more real than I have ever felt God to be.

ST. JOHN   God *is* love!

JANE   I hear you say it... but do you feel it? How can someone who has no understanding of their own heart talk of such things without them sounding hollow?

A beat. ST. JOHN appears hurt.

Perhaps if you had experienced it; if you had looked at someone, even for an instant, and felt safe within your own

159

vulnerability you might understand me when I say that I would travel with you as a sister, but to marry you... to marry you would kill me.

A beat.

I'm sorry.

ST. JOHN   You'd throw your life away?

JANE   Not at all!

ST. JOHN   Return to Mr. Rochester then?

JANE does not respond.

This is love for you, is it? This... *sin*... is your love.

JANE   I see the love before the sin. Clearer now than I ever have.

ST. JOHN   *(Quoting)* Watch and pray that you may not enter into temptation. The spirit is willing but the flesh is weak."

JANE   Matthew. Verse 26.

A beat.

Good bye St. John.

ST. JOHN   I shall remember you in my prayers.

JANE   I hope you do.

ST. JOHN exits. Music.

> *(To audience)* I watched him stride, upright and with purpose, down the stone path to the stile. Saw him climb it... then he disappeared from view. I never saw him again.

The stage is reconfigured around JANE to form a coach.

> I bid a frank and tearful farewell to my sisters, both of whom thought St. John mad for trying to persuade me to accompany him. By late afternoon I was clearing the little cottage, and at first light I walked into the village. I was going home.

FIVE enters. He is a COACHMAN. JANE sits and the COACHMAN makes as if setting the carriage in motion.

COACHMAN   Where to, ma'am?

JANE   Thornfield Hall.

COACHMAN   Right you are...

He spurs the horses and turns to her. The carriage moves off.

> Beautiful part of the world.

JANE   It is.

COACHMAN   I used to work there, you know.

JANE   At Thornfield?

COACHMAN   The late Mr. Rochester's butler.

A beat. JANE catches her breath.

JANE Late?

COACHMAN That's right. Not the present Rochester; his father.

JANE Oh!

COACHMAN Shame what happened there.

JANE I know.

A beat.

Is Mr. Rochester still living at Thornfield now?

COACHMAN No, ma'am; no! I suppose you're a stranger to these parts, or you'd have heard what happened last autumn.

JANE I've... been away...

COACHMAN Thornfield's a ruin.

JANE I beg your pardon?

COACHMAN Burnt down last harvest time. Saw it myself.

JANE It can't have.

COACHMAN Overnight. By the time the engines arrived from Millcote... nothing worth saving.

Music. As JANE sits, horror growing on her face, we hear lines charting her relationship with ROCHESTER overlapped; mixed

162

in with the sound of his laughter and the repeating of her name. We hear the sound of flames building; perhaps a sequence reliving the fire at Thornfield.

JANE   Could we go a little faster?

COACHMAN   You're not missing anything at this pace.

JANE   I'll pay.

COACHMAN   Ma'am, there's nothing left –

JANE   Please.

COACHMAN   Yaah!

COACHMAN makes as if whipping the horses. Music. COACHMAN and JANE stand as the space is reconfigured. It looks sparse and broken. COACHMAN exits.

JANE   *(To audience)* I sat among the ruins. I might as well have been sitting in the blistered chambers of my own heart. At dusk I walked into Millcote. Stayed a night at the George Inn and asked the locals about the fire. The only consistent answer I received was that Mrs. Fairfax had retreated to Ferndean, Mr. Rochester's other property.

FAIRFAX enters. She is rearranging chairs. Looks up as JANE turns.

FAIRFAX   Can I help you?

JANE just looks at FAIRFAX, allowing her return to sink in.

(*With a little recognition*) Jane?

JANE   Hello Mrs. Fairfax.

FAIRFAX pulls JANE into her arms in a warm embrace. Reads JANE's expression.

FAIRFAX   You heard then.

JANE nods.

Best we can guess it, *she* started the blaze.

JANE   I see.

FAIRFAX   The master was... after you left. He. Didn't take it well. Slept. Drank. Sent Adèle away.

JANE   She's not here?

FAIRFAX   No, thank heaven – the fire was started in her bedroom. The two puppets. William saw her tearing down the corridor, one blazing in each hand; the little bedroom burning behind her.

JANE   Where was Grace?

Pause. FAIRFAX looks down.

Did she...? (*kill her*)

FAIRFAX   We don't know. Some nights when her own demons became too difficult to entertain, Grace would take a gin. And Bertha – cunning as a witch – would steal

her keys, though... whether she did for
Grace or the fire took her...

The sound of flames underscore.

Bertha got to the roof; roaring like a she-
devil. Thornfield's all Halloween orange
and chimney red by now. We saw it from
the yard.

JANE And Mr. Rochester?

FAIRFAX He was up there. Course he was.
Screaming; pleading – reaching for her.
Couldn't hear what was said over the
blaze, but... looked like he might talk her
in for a minute... then she went. Head
over heels like a rag doll. Landed on the
driveway. Wouldn't have felt much.

A beat.

He came back through the house. Them as
were trapped inside; he freed the lot of
them. Wouldn't leave a soul. Then – went
back for Grace Poole, and... that was
when the roof collapsed.

JANE No.

A beat.

No. I was told... he's alive. Isn't he?

FAIRFAX He is. But...

ROCHESTER *(Off)* Who are you talking to?

165

ROCHESTER enters. FAIRFAX guides him to a chair.

FAIRFAX   You have a visitor.

ROCHESTER shakes his head.

ROCHESTER   I don't want anyone.

FAIRFAX   I think you might – *(change your mind when you find out who)*

ROCHESTER   *(With fury)* I don't want anyone!

FAIRFAX gestures that she and JANE should leave but JANE shakes her head. Another moment of understanding and FAIRFAX exits. Music. JANE watches ROCHESTER in his chair for a moment, before:

Are you still there? Mrs. Fairfax? Get me a little water.

JANE approaches him. She wipes a tear from her cheek.

JANE   There is no water, sir. None that quenches thirst.

ROCHESTER starts at the voice.

ROCHESTER   No; no... who is that? What sweet madness has seized me?

JANE touches ROCHESTER's cheek.

Jane!

They surge together, clinging to each other desperately.

Do you see me?

JANE   I see you.

ROCHESTER   I was... I've been so... how can you bear it?

JANE doesn't move away.

JANE   Beauty is of little consequence. Sir.

She kisses him. Their embrace is more passionate than ever before. Music. The stage is reconfigured around the interlocked pair; finally resembling the opening image. In a piece of choreography, TWO exits and JANE returns to the window, diary in hand. Music underscores.

JANE   *(To audience)* Reader, I married him. It was a quiet wedding; just the parson, the clerk, Edward and I. After, I wrote to Diana and Mary. Both were thrilled for me. St. John... I heard from some six months later. He did not mention the marriage in the letter, but the tone of it was kind.

A beat.

Edward had sent Adèle to a miserable school in the countryside – he admits his choices were clouded by the heart-sickness shared by us both. Using my independent means I found somewhere far more suited to her character. She's nineteen now and engaged to be wed herself. We write frequently. Her English is now far better than my French.

167

A beat. JANE stands.

> In the ten years since our own union,
> Edward has regained the sight in one eye,
> though the other sees light and dark only.
> We have a son; the very likeness of his
> father. Though perhaps not with his
> temperament. And I... have found the
> true beauty and serenity in that life has to
> offer... because I was free to share it. And
> that freedom has meant the world.

ROCHESTER enters.

ROCHESTER   Well, Jane?

She turns and looks at him.

> Have you seen enough?

JANE   I think I've changed my mind.

ROCHESTER   Oh?

JANE   Let's leave it standing.

ROCHESTER   It's a ruin.

A beat. JANE goes to him. He holds her.

JANE   No it's not.

*They kiss, then both stare out into the distance as the music swells.
Lights fade to black.*

The End